MW00641637

My Word is like a Fire

SHINING LIGHT ON THE SOUL

ALISON VEAZEY • KERRY L. SKINNER

My Word Is Like A Fire

Alison Veazey   Kerry L. Skinner

My Word Is Like A Fire
Copyright © 2019 by Alison Veazey and Kerry L. Skinner
Think LifeChange Institute of Biblical Counseling
www.thinklifechange.com

Library of Congress Cataloging-in-Publication Data

Skinner, Kerry L., 1955–
      My Word Is Like A Fire/Alison Veazey/Kerry L. Skinner, 1st edition
         p. cm.
      Includes bibliographic references.

      ISBN 13– 978-0-9648743-8-1

1. Personal Growth–Religious aspects–Christianity
2. Counseling–Biblical teaching

All rights reserved. Printed in the United States of America. No part of this book may be used or reproduced in any manner whatsoever without written permission except in the case of brief quotations embodied in critical articles and reviews. For more information address:

www.thinklifechange.com

Unless otherwise indicated, all Scripture quotations are taken from *The Holy Bible, New King James Version.* © 1982 by Thomas Nelson, Inc. Used by permission of Thomas Nelson, Inc.

DEDICATION

God has been so gracious in allowing us to serve Him. We know that without His guidance there would be no book. This work is the result of the Holy Spirit's direction as to what should be written and how we should approach the subject. May God be glorified as He uses these words to help others.

ACKNOWLEDGEMENTS

Special thanks to Elaine Skinner for allowing us to share her in-credible stories of God's activity.

Also, thanks to Glenda Stelly (Alison's mom) for her willingness to share God's work through her life.

Thank you Chloe Skinner (Kerry and Elaine's granddaughter) for helping with the editing process.

Thank you Hannah Mergist (Alison's daughter) for very helpful insights given through editing.

INTRODUCTION

And this is eternal life, that they may know You, the only true God, and Jesus Christ whom You have sent.
John 17:3

Alison and Kerry

There is an idea today that if a prayer is uttered to receive Jesus in our hearts then our eternal destiny is heaven and life continues on as normal. This thought is far away from the heart of God. Eternal life is not reaching heaven at death, eternal life is knowing the only true God and Jesus Christ His Son. Tucked away in the pages of God's Word is a lifetime of treasure that keeps a child of God occupied all the days of his life. Yet, it is clear that many children of God have strayed away from the treasure of His Word. Many believe that what is needed for life is found in this world. They abandon the understanding that God's Word is the only answer for changing a heart of stone to a heart of flesh. They miss the insight into the abundant life in Jesus which delights the heart.

Some believe that because we come from different backgrounds and that we are dissimilar, the only way for us to connect is to understand where we came from. As you embark on reading the pages in this book, you will hopefully realize that this idea is not true. We have two completely different backgrounds, and are from two completely different generations. God created a path that brought us together for His purposes. The common ground that knit our hearts together for ministry has nothing to do with background and everything to do with a life surrendered to the Word of God. We have a good friend in common–Jesus Christ! Spending time together and sharing the truths that God reveals is a stronger common ground than any background. We have a desire to share our friend Jesus with you through what He has done in our lives. When you read our testimonies and illustrations the hope is that you see God and not two people. Everything shared is a living testimony of who God is and the power that He still holds today.

Kerry was born in 1955 in Clarksville, Texas, and was raised in a pastor's home. Kerry was consistently educated and taught the Word of God. Alison was born in 1979 in Abbeville, Louisiana. She was not raised in the Word of God and did not come to true knowledge of God until her salvation at age 26. They were born 24 years apart in completely different cities and states and were raised in completely different types of households. In 2015 God decided to bring their lives together for His purposes.

How is it that two people so different can come together with the same mind and heart?

When you take a look at the disciples and prophets in Scripture you see that they are all different. It seems that many focus too much on the fact that people are different and not enough on the fact that God has been the same from the beginning. So much time is spent on learning personalities, and so little time is spent on learning and knowing the One True God. The mind of Christ is what brings us all together with one common goal, which is to develop in our walk with Him.

It is fascinating how God brings completely different people together for His purposes. God does use our differences for His glory. But our greatest learning comes when we understand the difference between us and God.

Open His Word and find Him.......This is eternal life!!

Alison Veazey and Kerry L. Skinner

BURNING THOUGHTS

At the end of each chapter you will see a special section called, "Burning Thoughts." These thoughts relate to the Scripture printed at the beginning of each chapter. In each chapter God speaks through His Word. Sometimes, the truth is missed if our spiritual ears are clogged. The fire of God's Word burns away everything that goes against the Truth. These burning truths come from reading God's Word, sitting in His counsel, and hearing from Him. Allow these burning thoughts to ignite in your heart and burn away all things that are contrary to the Scripture.

God has been teaching Kerry how to walk with Him for 57 years. Developing a relationship takes time, effort, and commitment. As I have sat under Kerry's teaching, I have witnessed the value of a strong connection with God. Kerry has shown me his quiet time journals that he has compiled since 1981. The burning thoughts at the end of each chapter comes from Kerry as he read the verse of Scripture, sat in God's counsel, heard from Him, and then journaled what God shared. The goal of these burning thoughts is to teach the reader how to read Scripture and hear from God in a life changing way. It is not enough to read the Word of God and miss the application to our personal life. Take the time and meditate on these thoughts and allow the Word of God to burn in you and to change you by the truth of His Word.

Alison Veazey

My Word Is Like A Fire

Contents

Section One

The Word of God

Chapter One

God's Word: Is Like a Fire

"Is not My word like a fire?" says the LORD, "And like a hammer that breaks the rock in pieces?
Jeremiah 23:29

Fire!-Alison's Testimony

As I sit to begin writing about the environment I was raised in–I pray, "Lord help me to share the parts that You want me to share, the parts that glorify Your name." As I pray this while overlooking a man-made lake in Cleveland, Texas, I see an alligator swim up to the bank. The alligator slowly sinks in the water where only his head is peeking through. While watching this God begins to bring my childhood environment into memory. In thinking on these memories I recognize that something is different. I begin to see things never revealed before. I see my life through my Father's eyes.

I was raised in a small town in south Louisiana. This area of Louisiana is known for delicious food, friendly people, and swampy terrain. What distinctly comes to mind is the wonderful home cooking. I have yet to find a place that has food as delicious as south Louisiana. I think of my grandma in the kitchen cooking us lunch as my cousins and I return from a morning of playing outside. After lunch we would head back outside and play until dinner. My grandfather was a farmer and my family lived on the same property as my grandparents. On the farm we had a variety of animals: cows, chickens, ducks, horses, and pigs. I remember the land being spacious and open which allowed us so much freedom to run around and play. While our property was spacious, my brothers, cousins, and I always knew the limited area in which we were allowed to play.

I have two older brothers and fourteen cousins. Our weekends consisted of family cookouts and spending time together. The whole family would come over and eat wonderful food and play baseball. My grandfather was a baseball coach and most of my brothers and cousins played baseball at one time or another. My family was extremely family oriented. We held high regard to maintaining a close knit family, not only with immediate family, but also with our extended family.

Wonderful memories of the environment in which I was raised come to mind. But there is one major element that I cannot ignore, I did not have a relationship with Jesus Christ. In fact, I did not even know what that meant. My mom raised me and my brothers in the Catholic church. I was baptized as a baby and had my First Communion there. I never knew what it meant to have a personal relationship with Jesus Christ. It's important to understand that when I was two years old my parents divorced. During the difficult time of divorce, my mom started to pull away from the Catholic church. Though I did make the required sacraments, I did not have a strong memory of practicing Catholicism.

What I do remember strongly is my rebellious nature. I was the youngest of three children and the only girl, so to say I was spoiled is an understatement. One particular vivid memory has never left me. When I was in the first grade I did not want to go to school. My mom told me that I was going to school. In my rebellious nature I threw a huge tantrum and refused. She decided to put me in the car and drive me to my grandparents house so my grandfather could help her with the current situation. As she was driving down the driveway of their property, I opened the car door and jumped out of the car. I did receive discipline from my grandfather that day and he took me to school. This nature of rebelliousness and disobedience continued to increase with age.

At the age of eighteen I became pregnant outside of marriage and gave birth to a baby girl. My life continued in the way in which I wanted to go, completely satisfying my sinful nature. I married at age twenty-four and continued that lifestyle. My husband and I had a baby boy after two years of marriage. I became a stay at home mom. One day shortly after I had my son, I was invited to a Bible study by my sister-in-law. I was more than thrilled to attend because I looked forward to a few hours with someone watching my baby. Little did I know what would happen at that Bible study. That was where I met My Lord and Savior Jesus Christ.

The particular Bible study I attended had very intense homework assignments. I am so grateful that was the case. As I began to read the Bible, God began to reveal Himself to me and show me what He saved me from during my childhood. Not until I began working on this book did I recognize the work of the Lord on my life before I even knew Him. Come with me and I will take you back in time to two major events that have shaped my life.

Salvation from Fire

As you come with me, we enter into my brother's bedroom when I was fourteen years old. I am asleep and as I wake up I wonder, "Why is it so hard to breathe?" I get up out of bed and run to the door. As I grab the knob to exit I can barely touch it because it is so hot. The hot door knob is a message to GET OUT. I run to the window and climb out. As I run around the house all I see is FIRE. Large engulfing flames are destroying my entire house. It is hot and it is very large. I run all the way to the edge of the property around the engulfing flames. As I make my way around the property I see my grandfather on his knees with a water hose. He sees me and at that moment realizes we are ok. He shouts, "Call the fire department!" I run to my grandparents house and call the fire department. By the time they arrive there is nothing left of the house. It has burned to the ground.

Have you ever witnessed that type of fire? The kind that destroys everything in its path. Fire is all consuming. Once it touches a source that allows a spark it begins to grow and as it grows it consumes everything in its path. When I received Jesus into my life, God reminded me that while that fire consumed my entire house–I walked away without even a scratch! As I sit here taking you back in time with me, I hear God speak to my heart, "I was with you Alison, before you ever knew Me."

(Staff photos by Chris Gaffga)

Abbeville Fire Department officers Cpt. P.J. Abate and George Choate

Fire destroys home south of Abbeville, spares residents

By CHRIS GAFFGA
staff reporter

Fire destroyed a home south of Abbeville Tuesday, spreading quickly through the house despite a light rain and the efforts of firefighters.

The home, located at 1720 Pumping Plant Road, was a complete loss, according to Abbeville Fire Department Cpt. J.P. Abate. The residents of the home, Glenda Stelly and her three child-

ren were unharmed.

Stelly's father and neighbor, Otis Stelly, said that he saw the flames shooting out of a utility room window on the back of the one-story brick building shortly after 8 a.m.

Mr. Stelly said that he called to wake granddaughter Alison Richard, 14, who was sleeping inside. "I kept hollering, but I couldn't get in," Mr. Stelly said. Finally, he said, she jumped out the window.

The Abbeville Fire Department and firefighters from Meaux and Nunez responded to the call which came shortly after 9 a.m.

"When we got there, it was just about all gone," said Abate. Stelly estimated damages at $75,000.

Stelly praised the firefighters, who made an effort to save the western end of the house.

Abate said the fire was caused by an undetermined electrical source. He ruled out arson.

Abbeville Meridional, Wednesday June 1, 1994
138th Year · No. 108   1st House Fire

Early morning blaze injures three

Moderate burns, severe laceration suffered in fire

By ANGIE HEBERT
lifestyles editor

An Abbeville mother and her two children remain hospitalized today after falling victim to an early morning house fire on Wednesday.

Officials say Glenda Stelly and her two children: Alton Richard, 17, and Jude Richard, 23; sustained injuries when their Pui Plant Road home be ignited with flames shou.ly before 3 a.m.

Stelly and her daughter received moderate burns in the mishap. Her son was critically injured while attempting to escape the burning home through a window. He managed to flee to his grandfather's home next door to call for help. Richard cut an artery while climbing out of the broken window and was reportedly bleeding heavily while waiting for medical assistance.

All three were transported to Abbeville General Hospital by Acadian Ambulance. Jude Richard has undergone surgery for severe lacerations and is listed in stable but guarded condition in ICU at

An Abbeville firefighter takes a moment to replace his air pack before returning into the Stelly home

(See BLAZE, Page 3)

Blaze

From Page 1

AGH.

Stelly and her daughter were both transported to a Baton Rouge burn center to access the severity of their burns.

Firefighters from Abbeville and Meaux-Nunez responded to the structural fire which left the home totally destroyed.

Fire officials suspect the fire began with a short in a ceiling fan, but their investigation into the matter is still ongoing.

Abbeville Meridional, Thursday July 24, 1997
141st Year · No. 143   2nd House Fire

Allow me to take you back with me to the second major event that has shaped my life. Let's enter my house a few years later when I was seventeen years old.

As I wake up I hear my mom screaming and think to myself, "Why is my mom screaming?" I know I must get up and check on her. As I round the corner of the hall, I cannot believe what I am seeing. Flames–large engulfing flames–are taking residence in my living room. The living room is full of smoke and blazing hot. I see my mom standing on the other side of the flames in the kitchen. She is screaming and not making much sense. I think, "You must run to her!"

Have you ever touched fire? Some parts of the flame are hotter than others. Have you ever touched the hottest part? There is an intensity to the pain you receive when you touch the hottest part of the flame that is indescribable.

Let's return to the scene. As I see my mom through the fire I quickly realize that she is disoriented and does not know what to do. At that moment I choose to run through the fire. In my bare feet, I run over the hottest part of the fire while the ceiling is melting onto my shoulders. Adrenaline kicks in and makes it hard to feel anything until I reach my mom. My feet are in excruciating pain so I drop to the ground. The fire is raging and eating up all that is in its path. "Mom we have to get out of here!" With strength greater than I have ever known I stand up, grab my mom, and run for the door. We make it outside and again I drop to the ground. My feet are in intense pain as well as my shoulder.

My mom says, "What about your brother?"

I respond, "Oh yes! My brother is in the house too."

We begin screaming his name with no response. My mom is in a panic and runs to my grandparents house. I cannot stand so I begin to army crawl in that direction. When my mom reaches my grandmother's house she enters the kitchen. She slides across the floor in blood–my brother's blood. The ambulance arrives and immediately administers a morphine shot for my pain. The pain is so intense the shot goes unnoticed. As the ambulance begins driving to the hospital the amount of pain is simply unbearable. What is a 5-10 minute drive feels like an eternity.

When we arrive at the emergency room my brother and I are in the same room divided by what seems to be a sheet. He tells me he loves me and then he is wheeled away into surgery. The doctors then begin to work on me. They begin the excruciating process of cleaning my burns. This is the most pain I have ever felt in my entire life. I was seventeen years old when my house was destroyed by fire a second time.

As my mind returns to that man-made lake in Cleveland, Texas, God reminds me that He was with me, before I ever knew Him. We found out later that my brother had climbed out his window and was punching through glass in order to save my mom and me. A piece of glass broke and cut the main artery in his arm. My brother had surgery on his arm and is doing well today. In both events there was no loss of life but complete loss of both houses.

I wonder as you stepped back in time with me, are you able to see God? I know that this trip back through these memories have allowed me to see God's saving grace in a new light. He saved my life from fire that destroyed everything in its path–twice. I know He saved me for a reason and I submit to His will. I ask, "Lord help me to tell the story of how 'Your word is like a fire'" (Jeremiah 23:29).

Pain

Have you ever been burned by fire? Just a touch of the stove can bring about much pain. Consider several layers of skin being burned off the bottom of your feet. The burning of your skin leaves your nerve endings exposed. Just a slight touch on these open nerves is the most excruciating pain you will ever feel. The kind of pain that morphine will not even take the edge off. The highest dose of morphine that your body weight can handle will not be enough for the pain. It is as though you received no pain killer. The pain still feels exactly the same. There is simply no relief.

This is the type of pain the fire left behind. When I was in the emergency room the doctor immediately began to clean my feet to prevent infection. Several layers of skin were burned on my feet and the skin needed to be removed. The doctor was using scissors to cut the skin off, but the pain felt as though he were grabbing each piece and ripping it off my foot. Keep in mind I had the highest dose of morphine my body could handle. It did not touch the pain.

My feet were not the only place I had burns. Some of the burns left my nerve endings exposed. I remember clearly being in the ambulance on the way to the hospital and having the EMTs want to cover me with a sheet. The touch of the sheet to my nerves felt as though they were hitting me with a hammer. The first hospital we were taken to did not have the ability to provide the required treatment that we needed, so they transferred us to a burn unit at a hospital in Baton Rouge, Louisiana. Baton Rouge is roughly a two hour drive from Abbeville. We were transported by ambulance.

When we arrived at the burn unit the first task was to be completely scrubbed and sterilized. This is called debridement, a process in removing damaged tissue and foreign objects from a wound. The unit for burn patients is very strict in sanitation due to the possibility of infection. My wounds were very dirty due to my army crawling from my house to my grandparents house. My burns were covered in dirt.

I clearly remember being taken to a steel tub and being scrubbed. The pain was simply indescribable. It is extremely important to remember the amount of pain medicine in my system was the highest dose of morphine my body could handle. After the debridement we were placed in rooms. My mom was in a separate room from me. The rule of the unit is that patients must stay alone in order to monitor germs and keep the patient clean. Remember, I was only seventeen years old. Since I was a minor, the hospital allowed someone to stay with me in my room. I had family members who would stay with me, mainly my aunt, my mom's sister.

Every day consisted of a morphine shot and then a bath. This went on for almost two weeks. The doctor recommended skin grafts for my third degree burns, which consist of taking skin from another area of the body and placing it over the area of the burn. This required surgery. The doctor removed skin from my right leg and placed it over the third degree burns on my right wrist and my right shoulder. When I woke up from surgery the pain was completely gone.

This picture of covering brings to mind Christ's act on the cross–His blood being poured out as a sacrifice covers the sins of those who repent and believe:

> *"Blessed are those whose lawless deeds are forgiven, and whose sins are covered; Blessed is the man to whom the LORD shall not impute sin."*

> **Romans 4:7-8**

The burns that I endured were physical burns that brought pain to my physical body. Sin brings pain to our spirit. The only covering offered for this type of pain is the blood of Christ.

> *But if we walk in the light as He is in the light, we have fellowship with one another, and the blood of Jesus Christ His Son cleanses us from all sin.*

> **1 John 1:7**

God takes the blood of His perfect Son and cleanses us from all sin. What a precious gift. Once the Lord removes the sin and replaces the diseased parts of our heart with His heart the pain of sin is removed. Spiritual pain is real and can affect our lives even if we have no awareness of it. Let's not resist the cleansing power God has provided for us.

I could have resisted the cleansing offered by the doctors but that would have only promoted increased infection. Resistance to cleansing is much more painful than repentance.[1] Allow the Lord to be the surgeon of your spirit.

Think about the idea of my surgeon performing the skin grafts before the debridement and cleansing of my wounds. Think about the result had he covered a dirty wound with the new skin. What would happen underneath the skin? I can say that over the course of my Christian walk I have done this. I have tried to take truths from God's Word and cover my wounds before allowing God to remove the dirt in my heart. What happens to the heart when we do this–increased infection and no healing.

At this point in my life I had no spiritual awareness but that does not mean that I was unaffected by sin. Just because we are unaware does not mean sin is not affecting us.

---

1 Kerry L. Skinner. *The Joy of Repentance Workbook.* (Think LifeChange Institute of Biblical Counseling, 2011), p. 116.

As I look back and process the house fires, I see something clearer than I saw at the time of the fires. God's protection and leading were at work even then. After my skin graft surgery, I went home and went right back to my old way of life. There was absolutely no understanding of what my family and I endured and survived. There was no grasp of the gravity of what we lived through. I just went right back to living my sinful life. As I study and learn more about fire, I realize there is no reason I should be alive today other than God wanting me to be. He was in pursuit of me many years before I ever received Him.

Now as I realize the amount of destruction fire can cause, and more so how powerful it is, I want to fall on my face thanking the Lord for guiding me. I am engulfed by how much He loves me and the measure that He will go to save me. I know that it is not only me that He loves this much. He loves you just as much as He loves me.

Are you willing to walk through the fire? What compelled me to decide to run through that fire rather than jump through a window like I had done before? The love for my mom compelled me to run through the fire. The relationship drove me. How much do we love our Lord? Would we walk through fire for Him? Would we dare to open His Word every day and spend time hearing from Him? What do you believe about God's Word?

This book contains the stories of the activity of God in the lives of the authors as He shaped them through the years. We have experienced the power of God's Spirit, the love of Christ, and the joy of salvation. It is our hope that through our testimonies and the information provided in this book that you can look at your life and find God in the places where you never knew He was. We pray God will ignite a spark in your heart to realize that He is found in His Word, that He is His Word, and that all is created from His Word. His Word is a person–Jesus Christ. Our hope is that Christians will move from simply reading God's Word as another book, to recognizing that when we sit down and open the Word of God– we are looking into the face of God.

God's Word

I met Dr. Kerry Skinner and his wife, Elaine in 2015 when he was the pastor of a church that my family visited. My family ended up joining that church, and Dr. Skinner became my pastor. When my family joined the church, I hungered to learn more about God. Over the next two years, Pastor Kerry began to teach and challenge me to learn how to walk in the Spirit. He also helped me expand and grow in my understanding of sin and repentance. During the course of this time, I also became the director of the care center that Pastor Kerry had started at the church. I was a counselor there as well and attended all of the training provided.

God began to knit our hearts together and it became clear that He brought us together for ministry. Through this realization, we formed *Think LifeChange Institute of Biblical Counseling.* After forming *Think LifeChange,* Pastor Kerry stepped down as Senior Pastor, and he and Elaine moved from Texas to Georgia to begin this ministry full time. They both have been such pivotal teachers in my spiritual development. While Kerry is no longer technically my pastor, I believe he will always hold a place of authority in teaching me what God has taught him. I now call him Kerry, which is kind of strange, but I am getting used to it.

Over the past two years Kerry and I have traveled to different churches teaching on biblical counseling by using God's Word as a mirror to the soul. In doing so, I have shared my testimony several times focusing on my experience in counseling as well as sharing about the house fires in my teen years. One day I was spending time with the Lord and I came across this Scripture:

> *"Is not My word like a fire?" says the Lord.*
> **Jeremiah 23:29**

This grabbed my attention and I began discussing with Kerry what God had shown me. Kerry and I had already decided that we were going to start working on a book together. God revealed this Scripture and made clear the direction for our writing. God's Word connected Kerry and I, and we pray that in reading this book, He would place a hunger in your heart to open His Word and spend time with Him.

Is not My Word like a fire?

One thing I am certain of is that fire is extremely powerful. I witnessed it destroy two homes and take away all that was in its path. As I read the Scripture in Jeremiah 23:29, it was evident to me that God's Word is also extremely powerful and has a much greater ability than I can grasp. In order to discover how God's Word is like a fire, I decided to begin with a greater understanding of fire. I found a copy of the *NYPD Fire Manual*. This manual is used to train New York's firefighters and has 1298 pages regarding procedures, protocols, and a detailed description of fire, its characteristics, and effective ways to put out a fire. It seems logical that in order to understand how to put out a fire, one must also understand the conditions that are ideal for a fire to grow and spread. Here is an excerpt taken from this manual:

> People first learn about fire as children. They know that fire consumes fuel, needs air, and gives off heat and light. Normally, that degree of understanding is all that one needs. Firefighters, however, have to take their understanding of this process a step or two further. In particular, they have to know more about the chemical process that goes on, the methods of heat transfer a fire can use, the makeup and nature of the fuels, and the environment the fire needs. It is this knowledge that arms the firefighter to fight fire and win.[2]

God says that His Word is like a fire. Are Christians satisfied in knowing the basics of God's Word, or are we driven to have a greater understanding of the Word of God to be prepared to fight the battles ahead of us? If God's Word is like a fire, a Christian should know it like a firefighter knows his fire manual. It is important to understand that the fire manual we are discussing is a book that contains knowledge in regard to fire, while God's Word is a Person that desires an intimate relationship with you. The fire that God's Word provides will enlighten the mind, light the way, and melt away the resistance and rebellion of the ones who choose to be in relationship with Him. A Christian cannot be in relationship with God without spending time in His Word. God is His Word!

---

2 NYPD Probationary Fire Fighters Manual, Volume 1, p. 43.

What kind of relationship do you desire to have with God? One that is easy to put out, or one that will sustain you until your final hour on earth? Much like there are different stages of fire, there are also different stages in regard to spiritual development in relationship to God. The fire that God ignites in our heart through the Holy Spirit is not a fire that we want to put out. This is a fire that needs to grow and spread.

> *Then I said, "I will not make mention of Him, nor speak anymore in His name." But His word was in my heart like a burning fire shut up in my bones; I was weary of holding it back, and I could not.*
>
> **Jeremiah 20:9**

Phases of Fire

According to the *NYPD Fire Manual* the three stages of a fire are: the Incipient Phase, the Steady-State Burning Phase, and the Hot Smoldering Phase.

The Incipient Phase[3]

The incipient phase is the earliest phase of a fire beginning with the actual ignition. The fire is limited to the original materials of ignition.

The Steady-State Burning Phase

The steady-state burning phase (sometimes referred to as the freeburning phase) can generally be considered the phase of the fire where sufficient oxygen and fuel are available for fire growth and open burning to a point where total involvement is possible.

During the early portions of this phase, oxygen rich air is drawn into the flame, as convection (the rise of heated gases) carries the heat to the uppermost regions of the confined area.

The Hot Smoldering Phase

In the hot-smoldering phase of a fire, burning is incomplete because of insufficient oxygen to sustain the fire. However, the heat from the steady state burning phase remains, and the carbon particles and other flammable products of combustion

---

3 Ibid, p. 49.

are available for instantaneous combustion when more oxygen is supplied. Improper ventilation, such as opening a door or breaking a window, supplies the dangerous missing link — oxygen. As soon as the needed oxygen rushes in, the stalled combustion resumes; it can be devastating in its speed, truly qualifying as an explosion. Backdraft can be the most hazardous condition a firefighter will ever face.[4]

With each increasing phase, the firefighters job becomes much more dangerous and much more difficult. The incipient phase is much easier to put out than the hot smoldering stage and the risks increase in each phase.

Spiritual Phases

As Christians, our goals need to consist of spiritual growth that creates a fire in our hearts that is very difficult to put out. With each growing phase, the job of the enemy to extinguish our spiritual fire becomes more difficult for him. A maturing Christian has a fire that is not easily extinguished. Much like the developing growth of a physical fire being described in phases, the development of a Christian can also be broken down into phases. These phases are not determined by age or time, but by your level of obedience. Avery Willis, author of *MasterBuilder*, discusses the phases of a believer.[5] The phases are as follows:

Unbeliever

This first stage shows that our role as a believer is to be a witness and our task is evangelism. As believers, we must start the flame by being a friend to the unbeliever and look for the opportunity to present Christ.

For the message of the cross is foolishness to those who are perishing, but to us who are being saved it is the power of God.
1 Corinthians 1:18

And my speech and my preaching were not with persuasive words of human wisdom, but in demonstration of the Spirit and of power, that your faith should not be in the wisdom of men but in the power of God.
1 Corinthians 2:4-5

4 Ibid, p. 52.

5 Avery T Willis, Jr. *MasterBuilder*. (Nashville: Church Training Deptartment of The Baptist Sunday School Board, 1985), p. 16).

Spiritual Babe

In this second phase, an unbeliever has just received Christ and is now a spiritual babe. If we do not help the babe, he or she will never grow. Our role to the babe is to be a parent and our task is to help him or her develop. If the fire of God's Word is to flame up in the spiritual babe's life, some help is needed. We cannot force growth but we can provide help when one is receptive to growth.

> *But we were gentle among you, just as a nursing mother cherishes her own children.*
> **1 Thessalonian 2:7**

Spiritual Disciple

In this third phase, our role is to be a servant to the disciple and our task is that of a trainer. Once again we cannot cause the growth but we can cultivate the person to help them learn to get into God's Word so that the fire continues to grow.

> *Who then is Paul, and who is Apollos, but ministers through whom you believed, as the Lord gave to each one? I planted, Apollos watered, but God gave the increase.*
> **1 Corinthians 3:5-6**

Multiplying Leader

In this fourth phase, our role is that of a manager whose task is equipping the leader. It is important that the person not only be solid in God's Word, but that he or she does not stop their growth at this point. The leader must continue to grow in God's Word. As the person grows in the knowledge of and obedience to God's Word, he or she become multiplying leaders.

> *According to the grace of God which was given to me, as a wise master builder I have laid the foundation, and another builds on it.*
> **1 Corinthians 3:10**

> *...each one's work will become clear; for the Day will declare it, because it will be revealed by fire; and the fire will test each one's work, of what sort it is.*
> **1 Corinthians 3:13**

Co-Laborer

In this last phase, the fire of God's Word is burning to the hottest point and the person is now a co-laborer with the trainer. Our role in helping this person is to be an encourager and to give support as he or she continues to develop in the way God has designed. But remember, God is the one who is the developer, we are just the encouragers.

> *So then neither he who plants is anything, nor he who waters, but God who gives the increase. Now he who plants and he who waters are one, and each one will receive his own reward according to his own labor. For we are God's fellow workers; you are God's field, you are God's building.*
> **1 Corinthians 3:7-9**

> *For this reason I have sent Timothy to you, who is my beloved and faithful son in the Lord, who will remind you of my ways in Christ, as I teach everywhere in every church.*
> **1 Corinthians 4:17**

The fire of God's Word in our hearts is much easier to put out in the spiritual babe phase of development than in the co-laborer phase. While the *Hot Smoldering* phase is the most dangerous for a firefighter, the unbeliever and spiritual babe phase is the most dangerous for the Christian. Our greatest protection as a Christian is to continue to grow closer to our Lord and Savior Jesus Christ. It is in His hand that we are the safest. Spiritual maturity is our safety.

So I ask you what phase are you in? The truth is that you will not advance in spiritual growth without spending consistent relational time with God through His Word. The fire that God's Word provides will enlighten the mind, light the way, shape the believer, discipline the believer, and correct the believer. Will you allow His Word to develop you, to grow you in your walk with Him?

Burning Thought #1

But His word was in my heart like a burning fire shut up in my bones; I was weary of holding it back, and I could not.
Jeremiah 20:9

God told Jeremiah that His Word was like a fire. Fire was used to heat up a rock in order to release its precious ore. God's Word does not destroy a person, it just destroys the sin of a person. When God's Word is placed in a person's mind and heart, it begins to warm from the inside out. It is like a burning fire that cannot be held back. In Jeremiah 20:9, the prophet did not want to keep sharing the message that God had given him but he could not help it, he could not hold it back. Why? Because in his heart the Word was like a burning fire that could not be contained. He had to share it.

Focus on Christ

When you focus on Christ–The Word, you will receive Truth that penetrates your mind, heart, and soul. You cannot contain it! You must use it and share it. When you spend time with Christ, His Word will burn out the junk and purify the soul, so that you can receive more Truth. This fire is a good fire, one that warms the heart, cleanses the sin, and restores one to a perfect union with Christ.

Focus on Self

The other option is to focus on self. Fill your mind and heart with the desires of self and you will come close to getting what you want from this world. You may attain wealth, position, prestige, and success, with enough hard work. But if you do, Christ will not increase in your life. You will miss out on His wisdom, guidance, relationship, comfort, and security.

I pray you will seek the best thing in life–Truth through the Word!

Chapter Two

God's Word: Enlightens the Mind

But if they had stood in My counsel, and had caused My people to hear My words, then they would have turned them from their evil way and from the evil of their doings.

Jeremiah 23:22

Kerry

For years I had heard the Scripture read, "Be kind to one another..." (Ephesians 4:32). I grew up in church learning how to recite that verse. It seems to be a rather simple verse that most anyone could understand. Yet, after being offended by someone, I could not seem to be kind toward that person. I certainly knew the Bible verse with mere intelligence, but could not seem to live it out in kindness toward someone I did not like.

One morning while asking God to help me get over my offended nature, He pointed out this simple Bible verse to my mind. God used His Word to break through my mind to move it from simple knowledge to having an enlightened mind on the subject. It was as though God had come face to face with me and said, "Kerry, you can receive a kind heart from Me if you want to give in to My ways!" That morning, I understood the difference between knowing what the Bible says, and being enlightened to live by the Word in complete surrender. I understood this truth:

...the eyes of your understanding being enlightened; that you may know...what is the exceeding greatness of His power toward us who believe...which He worked in Christ when He raised Him from the dead and seated Him at His right hand in the heavenly places...

Ephesians 1:18-20

My learning to be enlightened by God's Word began in 1980. I was serving in my first full-time position at a church in Cleveland, Texas. My pastor was Ken Hensarling. He was a godly man who took me under his mentorship and began to teach me the ways of God.

About a year after moving there, he shared with me that he had been invited to a special training in Houston, Texas and that he could take one person with him. He asked me to go. I asked him what it was about and he said, "A man named Avery Willis has written a discipleship training program called *MasterLife.* He wants to introduce it to about 40 people as a pilot project."

Little did I know what intensity of training and depth of material I would be introduced to during that week. We met from 9 a.m. to about 9 p.m. for five days! It was incredible what I learned. It was as though my heart burned within me as I heard the truth of Scripture. God was showing me exactly what I needed to grow. Avery shared what God's Word means when it says,

> *"If anyone desires to come after Me, let him deny himself, and take up his cross daily, and follow Me."*
> **Luke 9:23**

I learned that the primary way to take up your cross is to learn to live in the Word. John 8:31-32 states,

> *"If you abide in My word, you are My disciples indeed. And you shall know the truth, and the truth shall make you free."*

I grew up in a pastor's home, was called to ministry, and was educated in a Baptist college. Yet, that week, I discovered that my mind had not been enlightened to what it really meant to abide in Christ. I knew I should read my Bible daily, but I saw it as more of a task and a discipline instead of the result of being in a deep relationship with Jesus–The Word of God!

Every night that week, I would get home late and wake up Elaine to share with her what I was learning. I had never known what it really meant to walk with God. I was so excited! My mind was being enlightened and renewed with each of the teachings from God's Word through the week.

Not long after the *MasterLife* training week was over, Pastor Ken led his wife, Elaine and I, and three other pastors and their wives through the six month intensive study of *MasterLife*. We memorized two verses of Scripture each week for twenty-six weeks and had to retain them and apply them to life. Neither Elaine nor I could get enough of God's Word. We were so spiritually hungry for the Truth!

For Christians, the Word of God is our source of truth and the instruction for life. Without the Spirit of God enlightening our minds, we have no understanding of the Word of God.

> *In the beginning was the Word, and the Word was with God. He was in the beginning with God. All things were made through Him, and without Him nothing was made that was made. In Him was life, and the life was the light of men. And the light shines in the darkness, and the darkness did not comprehend it. And the Word became flesh and dwelt among us, and we beheld His glory, the glory as of the only begotten of the Father, full of grace and truth.*

John 1:1-5, 14

The Word of God is a Person, the Person of Jesus Christ. To have our minds and hearts enlightened, we must develop a relationship with Jesus through the Spirit of God. William Hendricksen's New Testament commentary on John 1:1 states, "Christ is the Word of God in both [two] respects: (1.) He expresses or reflects the mind of God and (2.) He reveals God to man. According to John 1:1, the Word was with God in the beginning. The Word existed in the closest possible fellowship with the Father, and that He took supreme delight in this communion."[1] The Word of God was face-to-face with God in the beginning. Therefore, when we open God's Word and connect to His Spirit, we are face-to-face with God. While Hendricksen states that through the Word Jesus expresses the mind of God, the way to the mind of God is through fellowship with His Word–Jesus Christ through His Spirit.

---

1 William Hendricksen. *New Testament Commentary: Exposition of the Gospel According to John.* (Grand Rapids, Michigan: Baker Book House. 1953), p. 70.

Born Again-Alison

Kerry shared with me an interview that he had with Dr. Henry Brandt years ago regarding a project on which they were working. Kerry began by saying, "Henry, you said one chapter could be on 'You have to be equipped to draw on God's resources.'"

Henry responded,

> You are not born with the ability to draw on God's resources. You must be reborn. I was reminded of when I was a kid in the thirties. Congress passed the rural electrification law. That law said that everybody in the United States should have electricity. I watched that happen in my area. First a truck came along and dropped off some enormous poles and then went away. Then someone else came along and dug holes, placed poles, and then strung wires on them. There was a pole next to our house but it didn't make any difference to us because in order to draw on this electricity we would need to have our house wired.

When a person is born again the Spirit of God takes up residence in the heart and a spark ignites. Though the source of light resides in him or her, there must be proper wiring in order to tap into the source.

Henry Brandt shared,

> We had our house wired. All those wires looked funny. Now we could have light. We had to get used to a light bulb. I never saw a light bulb until then. You could turn the light on and off. You could put as many bulbs as you wanted in the house. The amount of power was limitless.

In hearing Henry describe the law of electrification, it brings to mind our spiritual need to be wired for connection to the source. Being born again and having the Holy Spirit reside in us is the beginning of that wiring. But our daily relationship with God through His Word provides the ongoing wiring and continued growth to tap into God's mind. In order for our minds to be enlightened by the light of God's Word, it is critical to understand that the unbeliever is not born with the mind of

Christ. The mind of Christ is developed through a heart that is willing to allow Him to remove the thought processes of the world and rewire them to the thought processes of Christ. This is only accomplished by opening up the Word and sitting in the counsel of the Lord.

The human heart is not born with a wire already tapped into the source of light provided by the gift of the Holy Spirit. According to Scripture, we are born into darkness due to the fall of man in the garden of Eden. We are all born as unbelievers–born of flesh. As an unbeliever, the mind is set only on this world. An unbeliever has a natural mind that is unable to accept or discern spiritual things.

Remember for a moment the spiritual phases that were discussed in the previous chapter. The first phase discussed was the unbeliever. In this phase there is no flame in the heart of the person. The unbeliever is in darkness and the light of God is not in them. So how does one move from the unbeliever to the spiritual babe? First they must receive the light. According to Jesus, a person must be born again.

> *Most assuredly, I say to you, unless one is born of water and the Spirit, he cannot enter the kingdom of God. That which is born of the flesh is flesh, and that which is born of the Spirit is spirit.*
>
> **John 3:5-6**

Godly Thinking

Where does Godly thinking come from? When I began learning under Kerry's teaching, he held a weekly training meeting for lay counselors at church. I attended that meeting every week. At that point in my life, I had obtained a Master's Degree in professional counseling and had almost seven years of experience in the counseling field. I believed I knew a thing or two about counseling. I was ready to learn, but had no idea what I was walking into. Kerry would lead us in discussion and share truths from one of the workbooks he had written with Dr. Henry Brandt. In the beginning, I often left those meetings very unsettled. He was saying things that did not always line up with what I had previously been taught. I was being challenged in my thinking. I did not just take Kerry's word for it, I would consult with God and spend time processing the truths being revealed in prayer. Every single time God confirmed that what Kerry was saying was true. Why was it true? Because the messages he taught me were directly from God's Word.

At that time, I had only been a Christian for nine years and still had a lot to learn. There were definitely concepts that I had learned along the way only to later find out they were not God's truth. I began to realize that there were times when I was sitting in the counsel of the world and not in the counsel of God. What enlightened my thinking was God's Word. Through spending much time in God's counsel, Kerry learned to teach God's message of sin and repentance. This is not what was happening in Jeremiah 23.

In Jeremiah 23, prophets in that day were speaking falsely and claiming that their message was from God. God boldly stated through the prophet Jeremiah:

Thus says the LORD of hosts: Do not listen to the words of the prophets who prophesy to you. They make you worthless; they speak a vision of their own heart, not from the mouth of the LORD.
Jeremiah 23:16

But if they had stood in My counsel, and had caused My people to hear My words, then they would have turned them from their evil way and from the evil of their doings.
Jeremiah 23:22

If these prophets had sought the Lord and stood in His presence, He would have provided His words for them to teach His people. "Is not My word like a fire?" says the Lord (Jeremiah 23:29). God can take a person's hard heart and melt it into a tender heart. His Word can bring a deep change of mind, heart, attitude, and actions. When the Word of God is spoken, it will challenge any worldly or false teaching that may be embedded in the mind of the listener. At this point there is a decision to make. Will you receive the truth of God's Word and allow it to change your mind, or will you continue in your own thinking? I must admit that to receive the truth that God was teaching me, I had to abandon the false thinking that I received. This is not always an easy process. Yet, I had to decide who I wanted to think on, God or the world. It is dangerous to doubt the Word of the Lord. Thinking on both God and the world will bring confusion to your mind. God says, "For My thoughts are not your thoughts" (Isaiah 55:8). God's thoughts are revealed to us through God's Word. In order to set our mind on Him, we must sit in His counsel and not just simply read His Word–but let His Word read us.

Wisdom

When God called Moses to lead His people out of Egypt, He provided everything he needed to fulfill the task. God also provided him with detailed instruction to teach His people on how to follow Him.

> *Then the LORD said to Moses, "Come up to Me on the mountain and be there; and I will give you tablets of stone, and the law and commandments which I have written, that you may teach them."*
> **Exodus 24:12**

> *Then Moses went up into the mountain, and a cloud covered the mountain. Now the glory of the LORD rested on Mount Sinai, and the cloud covered it six days. And on the seventh day He called to Moses out of the midst of the cloud. The sight of the glory of the LORD was like a consuming fire on the top of the mountain in the eyes of the children of Israel. So Moses went into the midst of the cloud and went up into the mountain. And Moses was on the mountain forty days and forty nights.*
> **Exodus 24:15-18**

While Moses was on the mountain sitting in the presence of the Lord, God provided him everything that he was to teach His people. The instruction was to teach the people exactly what God told him. Moses was not to make up a law and teach the people. Moses was to take the Words of God and teach the people. This was exactly God's desire in the book of Jeremiah–God wanted His leaders to spend enough time in His counsel to know what to say to His people. Moses sat in the counsel of the Lord long enough to hear God's Words and then took what He taught him to the people. Can you imagine being in the presence of the Lord for forty days and forty nights?

Take a moment to imagine what Christ does for us. He sits at the right hand of God making intercession for us. Picture it, Jesus is calling out your name to God and asking on your behalf for the will and ways of God.

...It is Christ who died, and furthermore is also risen, who is even at the right hand of God, who also makes intercession for us.

Romans 8:34

Kerry can remember his dad, who was a pastor, sharing many times about Jesus making intercession for us. Can you imagine getting to heaven and everyone knowing your name because they heard Jesus call it out many times as He approached the Father on your behalf? What a blessing to think about!

The same Jesus who makes intercession for us has made a way for every believer to sit in the presence of the Lord.

Therefore, brethren, having boldness to enter the Holiest by the blood of Jesus, by a new and living way which He consecrated for us, through the veil, that is, His flesh, and having a High Priest over the house of God, let us draw near with a true heart in full assurance of faith, having our hearts sprinkled from an evil conscience and our bodies washed with pure water.

Hebrews 10:19-22

Because of the blood of Christ and the power of His resurrection, we now can approach the throne of grace and sit in the presence of the Lord. Believers can sit in His counsel and receive heavenly wisdom for every earthly struggle. Our minds are enlightened when we sit in the counsel of God's Word and allow the power of God to change us. With the same instruction as God gave Moses, we then should teach others. If you desire for your mind to be like Christ, you must sit in the counsel of the Lord.

God did not ask Moses to come up with the law to share with His people and He does not ask us to come up with the way in which we need to live. He provided the way through His Word and His Spirit through Christ's death and resurrection. We now have a choice. We can continue to view God's Word as a book of knowledge or we can open it up and sit in the counsel of the Lord to obtain His wisdom. If you doubt the power of God, you too will be tossed about in life without any vision of the truth.

Double-Minded

If any of you lacks wisdom, let him ask of God, who gives to all liberally and without reproach, and it will be given to him. But

*let him ask in faith, with no doubting, for he who doubts is like
a wave of the sea driven and tossed by the wind. For let not that
man suppose that he will receive anything from the Lord; he is a
double-minded man, unstable in all his ways.*

James 1:5-8

In Jeremiah 23, God compares His Word to a fire. We have discussed
the power of fire, and through testimony shared what a fire is capable of
doing. In the book of James man's doubt is being compared to a wave
of the sea driven and tossed by the wind. Have you ever experienced
the power of a wave? Many of us have been to the beach and sat next to
the ocean enjoying its beauty. But, have you ever experienced a strong
wave crashing over you?

Kerry's wife Elaine shared her experience of the power of a wave.
She said that several years ago, she was at the beach with Kerry's aunt
and his mom. Kerry's mom and aunt were standing in the ocean with
their backs to the water. Suddenly a wave came and knocked them
down. They never saw it coming. How could they with their backs to
the ocean? They began trying to crawl out of the wave but couldn't get
out. The wave also knocked his aunt's glasses off of her face and they
were somewhere in the water. Now she was trying to fight off the waves
with no vision. Elaine had knowledge of the ocean and had an idea of
where the glasses might be. She went under the water wearing goggles
and found the glasses exactly where she thought they would be. While
the ladies did make it out, the illustration of what a wave is capable of
is hard to ignore.

Elaine had knowledge of the ocean and knew the concepts of cur-
rents. Due to this knowledge she was able to find the glasses. She also
knew that you should never turn your back on the ocean. Someone going to the beach for the first time may not have this same knowledge.
Others may have the knowledge but choose to turn their backs regardless. How many of us turn our backs on God?

Elaine applied this knowledge while in the presence of the wave. The
waves of life come time and time again. The confidence that only Christ
gives helps us face them. We are not tossed around and left without direction. To know the Word of God, we must sit in the presence of the Au-

thor and allow Him to give to us liberally. Wisdom provides the ability to know how and when to apply the Word of God in our lives. Elaine would have been no help if she had just stood at the edge of the ocean holding on to her knowledge. Learning to apply God's Word to our lives is what living in victory is all about.

Doubting the Lord is like turning our backs on God. Doubt is like the wave that knocked down Kerry's mom and aunt. It was tossing them around, causing them to be disoriented to their surroundings. They were unstable and could not stand. Have you ever been tossed around in your mind? It is a very dangerous place to be. There is no vision or clarity on how to get out. Sometimes, as soon as another wave comes, you are tossed again. This produces instability in the way we live. When you lose your footing due to doubt, you have opened a door to deception and will have no vision of the ways of God. The deeper we go in the ocean of doubt, the stronger the waves are and the more blind we become.

We must choose to have faith in the Word of God. When we approach God with faith and ask for wisdom, the Scripture says that God, "gives to all liberally and without reproach" (James 1:5). Wisdom comes from standing in the counsel of the Lord, which means to be in close deliberation, in an intimate time spent with God.

Renew the Mind

And do not be conformed to this world, but be transformed by the renewing of your mind, that you may prove what is that good and acceptable and perfect will of God.

Romans 12:2

Whose counsel are you sitting in, the world's or God's? You can only know the answer to this question if you understand God's Word. When you hear a truth from God's Word that does not line up with your thinking, you are challenged. But what if you receive counsel from the world and do not know the truth of God's Word? The world's counsel feeds our sinful nature. When we do not sit in the counsel of the Lord, we are not walking in His Spirit–we are walking in the flesh. To walk in the flesh is to be conformed to this world. The sinful nature desires what the world has to offer.

For those who live according to the flesh set their minds on the things of the flesh, but those who live according to the Spirit, the things of the Spirit. For to be carnally minded is death, but to be spiritually minded is life and peace.

Romans 8:5-6

To renew the mind is to line it up with the truth of God's Word. This begins with an understanding of human nature according to the flesh. If we cannot accept who we are according to God's Word apart from Christ, it will be very difficult to allow God's Word to burn away what the world has taught us. If we believe that our thoughts are God's thoughts even if we did not sit in His counsel, we have conformed to the world. Our sinful minds are enemies of God. The only way to renew that is by allowing the fire of God's Word to burn away the impurities in our minds and take our sin to Him in repentance. Are we willing to walk through the fire and allow it to burn away the lies that have been embedded in us by the world?

Remember what drove me to run through the fire for my mom–my love for her. The renewing of our mind requires turning our love from the world and placing it on God. It requires taking our minds through the fire and allowing God's Word to remove what is not of Him. Fire is hot and it can be painful if it touches you. The fire of God's Word is meant to save us, not harm us. That does not mean it happens without pain. God saved me from physical fire but it was not without pain. Allowing God to renew our minds brings new life, new purpose, and new direction. When our minds are set on Christ our lives will reflect the life of Christ.

You will see things others do not and hear things others will not hear.

Then He turned to His disciples and said privately, "Blessed are the eyes which see the things you see; for I tell you that many prophets and kings have desired to see what you see, and have not seen it, and to hear what you hear, and have not heard it."

Luke 10:23-24

The Mind of Christ

The prophets in Jeremiah 23 did not sit in the counsel of the Lord, and therefore did not have the mind of the Lord. These false prophets were speaking to God's people words manufactured from their own worldly minds, for their own purposes and not for the purpose of saving God's people from their evil ways. To speak words created by our own minds and claim them to be God's is an extremely dangerous act. This fuels God's wrath because it leads His people away from His salvation. Our mind, apart from God's Word, is enmity to God. There are many mind traps along the way that feed the lusts of our flesh. So to be anything but connected to the mind of Christ as a Christian is to step out of the protective path of God.

Christ had the same mind from the time before His birth all the way to the cross. Jesus was sent to the world wrapped in flesh for the purpose of saving His people from their sins:

> But while he thought about these things, behold, an angel of the Lord appeared to him in a dream, saying, "Joseph, son of David, do not be afraid to take to you Mary your wife, for that which is conceived in her is of the Holy Spirit. And she will bring forth a Son, and you shall call His name JESUS, for He will save His people from their sins."
>
> **Matthew 1:20-21**

Joseph received a Word from God that revealed to him exactly the purpose of the baby. As Christ entered the world wrapped in flesh and began to grow and develop, His mind was set on the purpose of why He was sent–to save His people from their sins. This mind was with Christ all the way to the cross. His death and resurrection was the fulfillment of His birth. The resurrection of Christ is the power of God to save His people from their sins. The purpose of Christians today is to point His people continually to the salvation and sanctification work of Christ's death and resurrection. This is the power of God and is found in the Word of God. The mind of Christ is the mind of God and as Christians we are called to this same mind and to this same purpose.

> Let this mind be in you which was also in Christ Jesus,
>
> **Philippians 2:5**

Therefore let us, as many as are mature, have this mind; and if in anything you think otherwise, God will reveal even this to you. Nevertheless, to the degree that we have already attained, let us walk by the same rule, let us be of the same mind.

Philippians 3:15-16

Therefore to continue maturing as a Christian and to continue developing through the spiritual phases we must strive to have the same mind of Christ. Christ's mind was set completely on the will of His Father and the purposes set before Him. Christ viewed the world through His Father's eyes and not through the eyes of man. How can this mind be accomplished without sitting in the counsel of the Lord? Without spending time in the Word? The Word of God is the mind of Christ. To have the same mind we must set our minds on the Word of God. Paul's plea to the church was that all would be of the same mind.

Now I plead with you, brethren, by the name of our Lord Jesus Christ, that you all speak the same thing, and that there be no divisions among you, but that you be perfectly joined together in the same mind and in the same judgment.

1 Corinthians 1:10

For "who has known the mind of the LORD that he may instruct Him?" But we have the mind of Christ.

1 Corinthians 2:16

Anyone who comes into the presence of a Christian should experience Jesus. That means that you should not receive one message from one Christian and a different message from another Christian. This is very confusing to an unbeliever as well as anyone developing and growing in Christ. Due to the lack of being of one mind, there are many divisions in churches today. The fire of the Word of God is quenched when we have these divisions. Picture a church where every believer had the mind of Christ speaking the truth of God's Word. Imagine the fuel feeding that flame and the complete power that would flow out of the body. In order for a Christian to develop through the spiritual phases there must be continual daily renewal from the mind of the flesh (world) to the Mind of Christ (God). This is accomplished by sitting in the counsel of the Lord through reading, thinking on, and applying His Word.

Mindful Love

As we continue to think on the mind of Christ, it is fitting to discuss the love of Christ. Throughout Christ's life and ministry in the Scriptures, we see a genuine love for His Father. We witness constant and consistent fellowship with the Father. Christ's relationship with the Father is the driving force of His entire life and ministry as a human. His obedience to God was based on His love for God. Jesus stayed mindful of His relationship with God and did nothing apart from the Father. It is clear throughout Scripture that Jesus would take time to commune, pray, and consult with His Father. Jesus always knew His assignment because He continually spent time in the counsel of the Father.

There is a wide spread message in our day–how much God loves us. While this is true and biblical, a question we would like to address is, "Do God's people love Him?" Do we love Him enough to walk through fire for Him? Our obedience to God illustrates in a real life example our love for Him. We obey the One we love and trust. Let's take a moment to reflect on the ultimate sacrifice of Jesus for us. He endured the cross to save His people from their sin (Matthew 1:21).

> *Then the soldiers of the governor took Jesus into the Praetorium and gathered the whole garrison around Him. And they stripped Him and put a scarlet robe on Him. When they had twisted a crown of thorns, they put it on His head, and a reed in His right hand. And they bowed the knee before Him and mocked Him, saying, "Hail, King of the Jews!" Then they spat on Him, and took the reed and struck Him on the head. And when they had mocked Him, they took the robe off Him, put His own clothes on Him, and led Him away to be crucified.*
> **Matthew 27: 27-31**

Matthew 27:32-44 continues to share the mocking and torment that Jesus endured during His crucifixion. The question that is brought to mind is this, "During this horrific scene where was the mind of Christ?"

> *Now from the sixth hour until the ninth hour there was darkness over all the land. And about the ninth hour Jesus cried out with a loud voice, saying, "Eli, Eli, lama sabachthani?" that is, "My God, My God, why have You forsaken Me?"*
> **Matthew 27:45-46**

The mind of Christ was not on the men tormenting Him. His mind was on His relationship with His Father. The ultimate pain for Jesus was loss of His intimate fellowship with His Father. Do we love God like that?

As I read through the scene of Jesus' crucifixion, I realized that I had very little recollection of my mom's testimony in regard to the second fire that we endured. So I asked her to share with me her memory of what happened. Here is her testimony.

I am not sure what woke me up but I thought that I had left the coffee pot on, because I smelled burnt coffee. I opened my bedroom door and a backdraft of fire came rolling above on the ceiling in the hall. I started screaming, "The house is on fire!" I am not sure what compelled me to run through the living room and into the kitchen. The heat was so severe and the ceiling tile was melting and falling on my back. I started screaming that I was on fire. I thought I was going to die. I asked God to please not let me die, because my children still needed me. All of a sudden I heard Alison yelling for me to follow her voice. Her feet were burned and she could no longer walk. I still felt like I was on fire so Alison told me to remove my clothes, which I did. I didn't want to leave Alison on the ground but I knew I had to go for help.

I was screaming for my son Jude because I thought he was still in the house. However, he had escaped through his window. He heard me screaming when I was in the house so he punched through the window and cut his arm severely. He ran to my mom's house and fell to the floor. He was bleeding profusely. When I arrived at my mom's house, I slid across the floor in my son's blood. All of a sudden I heard my niece on the phone with 911. For some unknown reason she had decided to sleep at the house. My mom and dad were at the hospital because my dad had leukemia. Soon after, a sheriff's deputy arrived. Once I saw that Jude's bleeding stopped, I ran outside to check on my daughter. The ambulance had arrived and she was crying. The EMT was cutting the melted ceiling from her hair.

The first ambulance took Jude and Alison to the hospital. No one had attended to me yet. Once they noticed I was burnt, they put me in an ambulance. My shirt was cut off of me and I was severely burned on my back. Once at the hospital, I was told Jude was in surgery. I could hear Alison screaming. Once again I closed my eyes and prayed for God to take care of my children. I know now just how much the Lord did for us that day. Not only did we all survive but my father woke up from his death bed and went into full remission from Leukemia.

As my mom shared this story with me, she told me that she did believe in God at the time of the fire. She believed Jesus died on the cross for sins. However, she stated that she did not have Jesus in her heart and did not have a relationship with Him. Yet, in her time of distress, she cried out to the Lord.

In my distress I called upon the LORD, and cried out to my God;
He heard my voice from His temple, and my cry came before Him,
even to His ears.

Psalm 18:6

It was almost fourteen years after this house fire that my mom came to know Christ. She followed in believers baptism at age 62 in the church where Kerry was the pastor. As my mom shared her recap of this story I realized that I had no idea that she had called upon the Lord during those fires.

As I process her testimony, there are several truths that God revealed to me. First, my mom's mind was set on her children. While reading her testimony, it was clear that her mind was on the salvation of her children–from those fires. And when I think back to why I ran through the fire, I realize that my mind was set on the salvation of my mom. At that time my mom and I had been in a relationship for seventeen years. Through those years we established a love that fire could not destroy. Little did I know what running through that fire would mean so many years later. For my mom and I, it was the beginning of God drawing us to Him to receive Jesus Christ as Savior and Lord. It means being in relationship with Him and one day being together in eternity.

The desire of the Father's Heart is the salvation and sanctification of His children from sin, no matter the cost. The Father's eyes are fixed on His people. As Christians, our eyes need to be fixed on the Father. Jesus provided that picture for us. His mind was not fixed on the Father's children, His mind was fixed on the Father.

> *By this we know that we love the children of God, when we love God and keep His commandments.*

1 John 5:2

So I ask again, "How much do we love God?" Do we love Him enough to obey Him, to fellowship with Him, to learn His ways, and to sit in His counsel? Jesus loved the Father unto death on a cross for the salvation of sins for ALL who receive Him. Even though Jesus knew the reason for His crucifixion and resurrection and that He was sent to "save His people from their sin," His mind in His final hour was set on the loss of His intimate fellowship with His Father. We must set our mind on God through a love relationship with Him and covet our fellowship with Him as the goal of life.

At the end of my mom's recap of her testimony she said to me, "Alison, the Lord set us on a new path that day." God had started to draw us to a relationship with Him and through that relationship desires to lead us in His light. A characteristic of fire is to provide light, and God's Word is like a fire in that it lights our way.

Burning Thought #2

Focus on Christ

But if they had stood in My counsel, and had caused My people to hear My words, then they would have turned them from their evil way and from the evil of their doings.

Jeremiah 23:22

Can you imagine standing in God's counseling room and having God as your personal counselor? He knows everything about you and your future. He has perfect recollection of your medical, mental, emotional, physical, and spiritual past. This is the absolute best source for all your counseling needs! Wouldn't you want this Person to be your Counselor?

Yet, in Jeremiah's day, even the local pastors would not take the time needed to spend with God. They were not interested in having their minds enlightened by God. Instead they spoke from what others said or what they thought up on their own.

What does it mean to stand in God's counsel? That means to compare what *you are saying* with what *God's Word says*. God's Word is the standard, not your best thinking. Too many today want their thinking to be their direction. They do not even know enough about the Word to understand the direction the Word gives for daily life. Many people do not see their life or family change because they did not take God's Word for it.

But just imagine, if you focus on life with Christ, He enlightens your understanding with His Word! When you do not know what to do, He is not confused, He knows what you need! Turn to Christ every day. Stand in his counseling room–His Word–and He will enlighten you!

Focus on Self

The alternative to standing in Christ's counseling room is to depend on your self! Think about it. Self is limited in knowledge, wisdom, memories of the past, and for sure has no idea of the future. Is this where you turn for counsel? If so, you probably worry all the time. Worry comes when you do not have all the information and you know you do not. Self is where many turn for help, but it does not mean it is the best counsel.

Chapter Three

God's Word: Lights Your Way

"Behold, I am the LORD, the God of all flesh. Is there anything too hard for Me? They shall be My people, and I will be their God; then I will give them one heart and one way, that they may fear Me forever, for the good of them and their children after them.

Jeremiah 32:27, 38-39

One Step at a Time

Alison

When we think on the electrification process story from Dr. Henry Brandt, we begin to process what life must have been like for Henry living without electricity. For Henry, it was what he knew and lived. It was not until he received electricity that he even began to understand what it was like to have light at the flip of a switch. Today, we are so acclimated to having electricity that it is horrible when it is lost. We learn to adjust to what we know. While Henry did not have electricity, his life was not void of all light. In those days lamps and candles were available to provide light. The difference is that a lamp provides less visibility than a house wired with electricity. Today when we flip the light switch on the entire room is filled with light.

Your Word is a lamp to my feet and a light to my path.
Psalm 119:105

God's Word is like a lamp and not a room filled with electrical lights. Scripture lights the way for you to know what to do next, but it is not like a spotlight that shines far into your future and lets you know everything that will be happening. Many want to see miles and years ahead in their lives. A lamp in the days of the psalmist was very small and made out of clay. It could be held in the palm of your hand. The small lamp and wick only gave enough light to see a few steps ahead. You could not find your way until you actively took the next few steps. When you obey God in what He shows you in the Word, He will show you what is next. Disobey, and you will be distracted, get off the path, and be susceptible to traps.

> *My eyes are ever toward the LORD, For He shall pluck my feet out of the net.*

Psalm 25:15

If a person was walking in the woods where he knew many animal traps were set, he would carefully watch where he was going. Why? So he would not fall into a pit or a trap!

Satan has many traps set for us. How do we avoid them? Do we avoid them by consciously and carefully watching for each trap? This passage states that if we keep our eyes always toward the Lord, then we will always be on a path that avoids traps.

Our salvation is not in our ability to avoid traps but in our total trust in the Lord. If we trust Him enough to keep our focus on Him only, He said he would pluck our feet out of the traps. When we obey Him with the last light He gave us, we are protected and directed to go the right way. God's Word will lead you away from traps and keep you on the right path. The Word leads you to safety by following Jesus.

> *Then Jesus spoke to them again, saying, "I am the light of the world. He who follows Me shall not walk in darkness, but have the light of life."*

John 8:12

God gives us just enough light to follow Him in the present. As you spend time in His Word daily, He gives you more insight into how to take the next step. Walking with God is a journey. You cannot discover everything in a day. A relationship develops along the journey of getting to know Him as you travel through life. Kerry's wife Elaine has been walking with the Lord for fifty-one years. Her life is a wonderful indication of how the Word of God shines light one step at a time. Here is her story.

Elaine's Story

I was born and raised in Lafayette, Indiana. My family did not attend church. Though I had a good home with good parents, there was no teaching from the Scriptures. We did not even say a blessing at meal times. There was no understanding of the true meaning of Christmas and Easter. We truly believed that Christmas was about Santa Clause and that Easter was about the Easter Bunny.

When I was three years of age, my dad built a house for us just a few miles out of the city limits. Shortly after moving into this house, someone knocked on our door and invited our family to church. The church we were invited to was a small church that was not yet complete. The people met in a basement which was the beginning of their church construction project. My parents did not accept the invitation to go to church but did allow their four children to go. Every Sunday morning, Bill and Minnie Collins would drive to our home, honk their horn, and wait for all of us to get into their beautiful, unmarred car. This continued not for just a few Sundays but Sunday after Sunday for years and years. They would pick us up, take us to church and get us to our Sunday School classes and then sit with us through the worship service. Then, they would deliver us safely home to our parents.

At the age of sixteen, I became aware of my sinfulness and my need for a personal relationship with God. With the help of a pastor's wife, I asked the Lord Jesus to come into my life and to be my Savior. This brought such joy and peace to my heart. I went home that evening after the service and with great excitement shared with my younger brother about what had happened. Little did I know that God was working on his heart too. He awakened the next morning and was so excited as he shared with me about "doing the same thing" that I had done. I remember being very surprised that he too had asked Jesus into his life. The reason I was surprised was because he did not go to church. I was a babe in Christ and did not understand that a person could be born again without being at the church. He too had confessed his sin and called on the Lord

Jesus to save him. In less than a year, my sister and my older brother both came to know the Lord.

From the time I came to know Christ, I began to pray for my parents to also come to know Him. My brothers and my sister also prayed for this. I remember my heart being so very burdened for them. I wept and prayed and continually requested for the people at church to pray for my parents to be *saved*. In attempting to comfort me, someone shared a passage of Scripture with me,

Those who sow in tears shall reap in joy. He who continually goes forth weeping, bearing seed for sowing, shall doubtless come again with rejoicing, bringing his sheaves with him.

Psalm 126:5-6

With renewed faith, I clung to that verse and continued to pray for my parents. Upon returning from a worship service one Sunday evening, my parents noticed that my eyes were red from crying. They asked me what was wrong. I told them I was worried about them not knowing Jesus. They told me not to worry, they would be fine.

That night I heard them whispering in their room. Their room was next to mine. They said, "We might need to stop her from going to that church so much because they are brainwashing her." After that comment, I was very careful about letting them see my grief and even more careful about sharing with them from the Scriptures.

I continued, along with my brothers and my sister, to pray for my parents. I found new ways to share the Gospel with them. I shared with them the many testimonies of the children I taught in Bible Study. When our son, Jason, was six years of age, he prayed to receive Christ as his personal Savior. I wrote my mom and dad and told them about his decision. My mother wrote back and said, "Tell Jason that we are very proud of him." I will never forget Jason's response. He said, "Mom, how can Grandma and Grandpa be proud of me when they still have not asked Jesus to be their Savior?"

About five years later, I was on my knees in front of our sofa weeping and asking God to help my dad to come to know Him. Then I started praying differently than ever before, I remember saying, "God, I want my dad, to be saved. I don't want him saved to make my life easier, and I don't want him saved because it would hurt my heart or hurt him to be in hell some day. I want him saved because I know You created him and he is Yours. I want him saved because I know You love him more than I could ever love him. Not for me, God, but for You." At that moment, I knew beyond a shadow of a doubt that my dad, would come to know Christ and that Kerry would be the one to lead my dad to Him.

My mom suffered from a heart condition and I helped to care for her. On one of my many trips to Indiana, I asked the Lord to open a door for me to share the Gospel with my parents. I had to wait for God to open the door. I was with them for about two weeks and then Daddy took me to the airport to fly home. I was disappointed that God had not opened a door for me to talk to them about Him. On the way to the airport my dad suddenly asked me a question. He asked, "Lainey, how do you know there is a heaven and that you can go there? I believe there is a God because years ago, me and my friend, Charlie, were hitch hiking. It started to storm, and we were stuck in the rain. I told Charlie that we should pray and ask God to give us a ride." He said, "The next car that came stopped and gave us a ride, and it was a preacher." I asked my dad if the preacher said anything to them about God. He said, "No, he didn't care about us because we did not live there and would not be members of his church." My heart broke! My dad then said, "I've been watching you and Kerry and how dedicated you are to God." I then shared with my dad how to become a Christian. Suddenly, we realized that we had missed the exit to the airport. We ended up at a military airport with a bunch of green army planes. Daddy finally found his way out of that area and got me to the airport just in time to check in, hug him, and get on the plane. I was the last one on board before they closed the door. I sat down in my seat and once again my heart was broken. Because the burden was so intense, I failed to see that God was working to bring my parents into a relationship with Him. The burden alone was proof of His working.

One Sunday morning, we received a call from my mom that my dad was in the hospital. He had passed out while making the bed. He needed bypass surgery, but there were complications. It was an eighteen-hour drive from where we lived in Texas to the hospital in Indiana. Kerry, Jason, and I left immediately. On the way to Indiana, we ran over a piece of angle iron that had fallen from a truck. We had just changed drivers prior to this happening, so Kerry was driving. Two tires blew out at the same time on one side of the van. Kerry was able to guide the vehicle off of the road. We were stranded in the middle of nowhere. There was nothing close to where we were and most businesses were closed on Sunday. This was before there were cell phones to make a call for help. As we stood looking around for our hubcaps, a very attractive African-American couple all dressed in white pulled up in a jeep. My first thought was, "God sent angels to help us." This couple took Kerry with them and left Jason and I with the van. Kerry came back with someone who could fix our vehicle. It was amazing how quickly this moved along and we were back on the road without too much delay.

We arrived at the hospital in Lafayette, Indiana and rushed in to see my dad. We hugged him, and they immediately moved him into ICU where they would put him on Life Support. My dad had no idea he was at death's door. He felt okay but just wasn't getting enough oxygen. He didn't know it was so serious. Kerry talked to the doctor and asked if he could talk to my dad. The doctor said this was too serious and that my dad was being given one hundred percent oxygen but his body was not absorbing it. The doctor told Kerry that he must put him on life support immediately! Kerry told the doctor how critical it was for him to talk to him before that happened. He convinced the doctor to let him have a few minutes with my dad. Being a minister, Kerry was allowed to stay in the room, and the doctor agreed to step out for a few minutes. Kerry shared the Gospel with my dad as me and my brother sat outside the room and prayed for Daddy to understand what Kerry was saying. My dad had no idea how critical his situation was. He felt good. As Kerry was sharing, my dad said, "Oh, I understand!" He then prayed to receive Christ. My dad lived for eleven days on life support prior to the Lord calling him home. He was a changed man and had peace in his heart. He wrote a note to me that said, "Thank you for coming for your mom and thank you for telling me about God."

During the next few years, my mom came to know Jesus. She started going to church on Sundays and to special events for women at the church. If she could not drive due to the weather, she would call her pastor to come and pick her up. She began to read the Bible during those years. My mother went to be with Jesus eleven years after my dad passed on.

As I look back on all that has taken place since becoming a Christian, I am amazed at all that God has done. His Word has been my guide and prayer has been strength to my soul. Psalm 121 is one of the first passages of Scripture shared with me as a new believer.

I will lift up my eyes to the hills–From whence comes my help? My help comes from the LORD, Who made heaven and earth.
Psalm 121:1-2

As we read the progression of Elaine's testimony, it is evident that God's light was present. The journey from the time Elaine was invited to church to the time of her salvation was three years. The journey from Elaine's salvation to the time that her dad received the gospel in the hospital room was twenty years and her mom received Christ one year later. How did Elaine stay on the journey? She did this by taking one step at a time using God's Word as her lamp and prayer as her fellowship with Him as a Guide to keep her on course. Through His Word and prayer, God developed in Elaine a heart that had the same desires as His heart. Through this, she was able to see the way on the road from His perspective. Because her mind was set on God, she was able to avoid the traps.

Elaine's love for God and her love for her parents lit the lamp that guided her along the path until her parents received Christ. Elaine simply stepped where God showed her to step. All of the waiting time was spent growing and developing in her relationship with God. God deepened Elaine's prayer life and her understanding of following Him.

Elaine did not learn everything and then decide to obey, she obeyed and received new insights with every step of obedience. This is the way established by the Lord. With every act of obedience, you take one more step in the ways of the Lord, and He in turn establishes a deeper relationship with you.

You get to know a friend by sharing your life together, talking, discussing the things of God, and praying for one another. This requires a journey together–not a day trip! Travel the country together, and you will learn much more than driving to a local event. To be enlightened by God requires an investment of time into His Word to discover His marvelous truths.

> *Oh, the depth of the riches both of the wisdom and knowledge of God! How unsearchable are His judgments and His ways past finding out!*
>
> **Romans 11:33**

Light Through Prayer

In Jeremiah 23:23-24 God says: *"Am I a God near at hand," says the LORD, "And not a God afar off? Can anyone hide himself in secret places, so I shall not see him?" says the LORD; "Do I not fill heaven and earth?" says the LORD.*

God fills heaven and earth and knows every single moment of our lives. God's ability is so vast that we cannot even know for sure where the start of Elaine's journey began. There are many details of the story that Elaine cannot know–only God knows. How many people were praying for Elaine and her family? What took place in Bill and Minnie's life that lead them to knock on Elaine's door and invite her family to church? Who sent the African-Americans? We will never know the answers to these questions.

God is the only one who knows every detail of every life involved in the journey toward the salvation of Elaine's family. The process involved many believers who God used to fulfill His will. The weaving together of every detail can only be accomplished by the One who fills heaven and earth. And He is near to us!

The words of this song are an incredible depiction of the power of prayer:

> *Our prayers break the boundaries of time and reach into eternity.*
> *Our children will live in the atmosphere of the prayers that we*
> *have breathed.*

Steve Amerson "Pray for the Children"[1]

One Way

Throughout Scripture, it is clear and evident that God provided the way for His people. God provided direction to the Israelites in the wilderness even when they left Him.

> *Even when they made a molded calf for themselves, and said,*
> *'This is your god that brought you up out of Egypt,' and worked*
> *great provocations, yet in Your manifold mercies You did not for-*
> *sake them in the wilderness. The pillar of the cloud did not depart*
> *from them by day, to lead them on the road; nor the pillar of fire*
> *by night, to show them light, and the way they should go.*

Nehemiah 9:18-19

The pillar of cloud lead them on the road by day and the pillar of fire by night to show them the light and the way they should go. God's Word consistently reveals the way in which you should go. He never leaves it up to us to know or decide on our own. He did not ask Moses to make up the commandments–He provided them! He did not ask the Israelites to find their way on their own–He provided the way! The New Testament reveals that God sent the Way when He sent Jesus to die on the cross.

> *Jesus said to him, "I am the way, the truth, and the life. No one*
> *comes to the Father except through Me.*

John 14:6

From the beginning of time, God has provided light in regard to the way in which He desires for His children to go. In the Old Testament, His presence was in a pillar of cloud by day and a pillar of fire by night.

---

1 © 1989 Dick and Mel Music

In the New Testament, and even up to our day, His presence rests in the life of Christ through the Holy Spirit revealed in His Word. No one will come to God without entering through His Son Jesus Christ by His Spirit. Elaine entered the narrow way when she received Christ as her Lord and Savior, she followed that with baptism and then surrendered her entire life to the call of God. With every single step she took, the Holy Spirit revealed the light of God's Word through prayer. Her direction was provided for all the steps she needed to take. Elaine committed to the journey God had before her by consistently staying in His Word and consistently growing and developing in her Walk with God.

> *Then Jesus said to those Jews who believed Him, "If you abide in My word, you are My disciples indeed. And you shall know the truth, and the truth shall make you free."*
> **John 8:31-32**

Over the course of Elaine's fifty-one year relationship with God, she has stayed committed to remaining in His Word. Through this commitment, Elaine's parents were able to see the light in her life and they were able to see Jesus. Eventually they came to the light. Through God's Word we are developed into becoming more like Jesus Christ. Without His Word we remain malnourished in our development in Him. To move through the phases of development discussed in Chapter 1 requires continued time spent in God's Word, allowing it to light your way, shape you, correct you, and discipline you to be molded into the only Way to God, Jesus Christ. Never forget that God fills all of heaven and earth, and knew the way of salvation for Elaine's parents from the beginning. As a believer, He knows the way of your life too. He has known the way all along. Are you ready to commit to the journey and follow God? Until you do, your way will be dim at best.

> *Jesus answered and said to him, "If anyone loves Me, he will keep My word; and My Father will love him, and We will come to him and make Our home with him.*
> **John 14:23**

Burning Thought #3

"Behold, I am the LORD, the God of all flesh. Is there anything too hard for Me? They shall be My people, and I will be their God; then I will give them one heart and one way, that they may fear Me forever, for the good of them and their children after them.

Jeremiah 32:27, 38-39

Focus on Christ

It is amazing that God sometimes has to remind us of His character. He asked the question to Jeremiah to make a statement, "Is there anything too hard for Me?" God certainly does not remind us of His character so that we can know how great He is. God reminds us so that we will remember, be assured, and have confidence that nothing is too difficult for Him.

Maybe you are going through a struggle right now as you read this book. Possibly, there is an obstacle, a problem, or a crisis that seems insurmountable. Most likely, it is impossible to see a solution without God's help. But do you suppose that the God who simply spoke the universe into creation could deal with the issues of your life?

God gave a strong but comforting Word to His people. He revealed judgment was coming because of their straying from Him. God told His people that one day all things would be corrected and they would again be His people and He would be their God. He would bring them back to their land and they would have a singleness of heart toward Him. No longer would they stray and follow others gods and their own thinking. With one heart focused on Him, they would have a healthy fear of God. He would do good things for them and their families forever.

Do you want this kind of walk with God? If so, stay focused on Christ by keeping your thoughts on His Word–with a heartbeat only for God.

Focus on Self

It is so easy to act like the people of God in Jeremiah's day. Just simply move away from God by not listening to His Word! When you do not stand in the counsel of God, you do not have the wisdom available to you from the God who created the universe. It seems that so many have lost the fear of God. People in our day are more afraid of what their friends think if they do not join in with the things of the world, than what God thinks if they do! Remember God's awesome power to dethrone you from your self is a simple act from God. This memory can be a healthy fear of God that keeps you from going astray.

Section Two

The Hand of God

Chapter Four

God's Hand: Shapes the Soul

And the vessel that he made of clay was marred in the hand of the potter; so he made it again into another vessel, as it seemed good to the potter to make.

Jeremiah 18:4

The Potter and the Clay

Kerry

Have you ever felt like your life was not shaped the way that you planned it to be? Maybe there were some areas of your life that you always wanted to improve, but you never quite achieved. Or maybe, many of you could say, "The things that I am doing in my life today, I never had any idea that I would be involved in." Maybe your life changed so drastically when you came to know Christ that you wondered where it is going to go from here. What is next?

At age nineteen, I was called by God to follow Him in full-time ministry. I really did not know what to do next, but I knew that I needed some kind of training. C. E. Wiley was a director of missions for the Indiana Baptist Convention and a member of the church where my Dad was the pastor. He suggested that I should go to college and prepare for the ministry. He was personal friends with Dr. Randy Davenport, the President of Campbellsville Baptist College in Campbellsville, Kentucky. C. E. made arrangements for us to talk with the President and consider attending there.

Things worked out for me to attend there but there was a problem. Elaine and I had very little money to go to college. I had been accepted as a student for the fall semester of 1975. I began working with a partner, and in May of that year, I began to make a large amount of money. I thought that I needed to keep working for a while so I could gather enough finances to take care of us when we would eventually go to college. I knew God had wanted me to start classes that year, but I decided I knew better than God and that I should work until December and start my classes in January of 1976.

I was trying to shape my life the way I wanted in my timing. As soon as it was too late to start in the fall semester of 1975, God took all my abilities away for making money. I lost my job and could not find another one. Finally, the only job I could get was sweeping floors at an auction barn. My pay was one dollar less than the minimum hourly wage. I couldn't pay the rent, the electric bill, or much of anything else.

It didn't take me long to say, "God, I get it! I messed up! I will start classes in January no matter what." December rolled around and I was deeper in debt. We had no money to move. A man in our church offered to help us. He drove his pickup truck and we rented the smallest u-haul trailer.

On the five hour drive, in the cold of January, we moved while it was snowing. Halfway there, the truck engine exploded. Our friend called someone he knew that lived about an hour away. We went there to spend the night. Finally, the next day we arrived at the college after dark and could not find anyone on campus who had the key to our little house that we were renting. I say a little house: it was called, "Hut #6." It was temporary housing from World War II bought from Fort Knox for married students housing at the college. Our rent was $55 a month and it included the rental of a stove and refrigerator!

When we arrived, I had $200 cash in my pocket and no other money in the bank. Neither of us had a job. We prayed and asked God to provide jobs. Before we left Indiana, I wrote a letter to our landlord and the electric company. I described how God had called me into the ministry and I had lost my job. I knew that I owed them and said in the letter that I promised to pay them in full as God provided. It is amazing that both answered and thanked me for the letter and said it would be fine to pay when we could!

God was shaping our lives to live by faith.

Are you really willing to be shaped by God and do anything that He wants to do with your life? People are changing careers many times in their lives. College students are finding out what their majors will be as late as their senior year. Some graduate and then go back for a different degree because they were not sure that they got it right the first time. We should ask God, "God, am I on the right path; have I made the right decisions at the right time; and am I right where You want me to be?"

Jeremiah was an unusual prophet of God. He was selected by God before he had even been formed in the womb (Jeremiah 1:2). His assignment was to Judah, but as is seen later in the book, he also spoke to Gentiles—making him a prophet to the nations. Jeremiah was just a young man, possibly in his late teens or early twenties, and claimed he was not experienced enough to speak for God (Jeremiah 1:6-9). God put the words in Jeremiah's mouth to speak on His behalf. Jeremiah never saw a convert and the message God gave him to deliver was always rejected. The message broke his own heart (Jeremiah 9:10). Though he was a priest, his message from God was opposite of the one the other priests were delivering without requiring an obedient heart. How would you like this assignment?

In Jeremiah 18, God addresses a nation of His people who had forgotten who He was. What a tragedy! If you recall when you first came to know Christ and realize the magnitude of the fact that the Creator of the universe came into your life—it is overwhelming! Can you imagine living today as though you had completely forgotten that moment when you were born again? That is what had happened with the nation of Judah. So, God had a Word for them in chapter 18.

The Potter and The Clay

A potter is a person who takes clay, shapes it, and molds it into some form that is useful. The way a potter molds clay today is almost exactly the way that it was done in Jeremiah's day. There are only three elements needed to mold a lump of clay. First, a skilled potter is needed to shape the clay. Second, the potter needs a lump of clay. Third, a potter's wheel is needed. As the wheel turns, the potter puts his or her hands on the clay and begins to mold it as it spins.

Once the clay is molded into the vessel that the potter desires, it is placed through a firing process. This process is needed to provide strength to the clay. Before the firing process, the clay is weak and easily broken. It is the potter's wisdom that allows him to know when to place the clay through the firing process. It is imperative that the clay is clean and all the stubborn spots are removed because, once the clay is taken through the firing process, the finished product will be that way forever.

God told Jeremiah to go to the potter's house and hear His words (Jeremiah 18:3). For all born again believers, God is our Potter. He is shaping our lives. We are simply the clay, and He is going to mold us into the vessel that He wants us to become. God is not interested in whether or not your life is successful by the world's standards, He is interested in how you look when you come out of the potter's house. He is interested in how you will be formed by the shape of His own hands.

Many people ask, "How do I know whether it is God working in my life or Satan tempting me? Is my own flesh bringing these pressures to my life?" There are all kinds of pressures that come our way. Believers think the pressure in their life tends to be more from Satan than from God. But realize, as a child of the King, God is the most active person in your life. God is the One who molds you; He is the One who makes you; and He is the One who works on every facet of your life.

God is also the One who decides when it is time to place you in the fire for strengthening. The trials of life are designed to provide strength to the believer. The stronger the faith, the stronger the believer is able to withstand the tribulations in this world. A believer refined through fire has a mind set on the ways of God. The Ways of God will always be better than our own way. God was shaping Kerry and Elaine for ministry and in doing so they were placed in the fire. Kerry's first response was to go his own way. The way in which he thought was a better way. Through Kerry's resistance God increased the fire. The experience of the fiery trial strengthened the faith of Kerry and Elaine to continue to pursue God. It taught them not to trust in their own way. Do you trust that the Potter knows exactly when to place you in the firing process? It is crucial that the Hand of God is received as a blessing to create the vessel that God intends to create. The Master knows exactly what you need to be. Allow Him the ability to shape, mold, and strengthen you for the purpose that He has for you.

Since the Heavenly Father is at work in your life, you need to pay attention to what is happening moment-by-moment and day-by-day. Pay attention to how the Heavenly Father is shaping you.

A potter would also locate his house near a place called a potter's field. This was a place where he could not only find good clay to work with, but also a place to discard those things that did not turn out so well. Have you ever tried to make something only to have to throw it away? Maybe a new business or a decision about how you would make your living. Well, a potter also had to make a decision about what to make. He or she started with the best clay that could be found, a sedimentary clay that had been ground through the process of pressure over time. But even the best clay always had some little pebbles left in it. The potter would take that clay and put it on a wheel. As it was turned the pressure of the hands of the master would begin to shape the clay.

God does that for us. He has direct contact with us. He puts His Hands on our lives. He begins to put pressure where it is needed. Have you ever felt the pressure of God's Hand? Have you ever prayed for patience? "Lord, give me more patience." That is the most opportune time for our Heavenly Father to put pressure on your life.

As the pressure of the potter's hands begin, it forms the clay into the kind of vessel that the potter had in mind. God is really not interested in what you might have in mind for your life. He is interested in what He has in mind. The potter never asks the clay, "Clay, what do you want to become? Would you like to be a cup, or a vase, or a bowl?" Before beginning a vessel, a potter has in mind what that lump of clay is to become. When God saved you, He had a purpose in mind. He knew exactly what He wanted to do to form you into what He wanted you to be, and He began to put pressure on your life to form you the way He wanted to form you. The clay simply submits to the hands of the potter. Do you simply submit to anything God asks of you? You have no mind about it at all, no impressions, no will, you just submit. Correct?

The Scripture states,

And the vessel that he made of clay was marred in the hand of the potter; so he made it again into another vessel, as it seemed good to the potter to make.

Jeremiah 18:4

When God is molding your life by putting pressure on you to shape you, He is not experimenting. He is not wondering what He can make of your life. He knows the right formula, shape, and direction for you.

Sometimes when the potter shaped the clay it suddenly was marred. What does that mean? When a potter works with clay, within the substance itself, there may be a gritty or stubborn spot. Maybe a pebble or a little stone is under the surface of the clay. That spot has to be worked out of the clay for the vessel to develop properly. As the wheel spins around and the master puts pressure on the clay, the pressure of the hand may encounter that little pebble in the clay. A moment of pressure on a stubborn spot puts a streak all around the vessel. The vessel is marred or injured. It was not the pressure of the potter's hand that caused the problem. It was the stubborn spot in the clay. Do you have any stubborn spots in your life? Maybe your stubborn spot sounds like this, "I am moody and I am pouting," or "I am aggravated," "I am stubborn," "I am impatient," or how about this, "I am a complaining person who is ungrateful for my life." You can get rid of those spots if you will release them. But you can also hold on to them as long as you want. If the potter cannot get the clay to release the stubborn spot, he or she will crush the vessel and start all over.

If there is an area of life that you will not obey God in, He will put more pressure to shape you. But if you resist and go into disobedience again and again, He may leave you as a marred vessel and have to set you aside. Have you discovered that God will let you be miserable if you want to be miserable? Have you discovered that God will let you make wrong choices if you want to make wrong choices?

Many are resisting the activity of God in their lives. God wants you to change any area of disobedience into obedience. That is why He calls you to repentance. But if resistence lasts too long, there comes a time when the potter just sighs, smashes the clay, and begins all over.

While teaching at a conference center in New Mexico, a lady talked to me after one of my sessions. She said, "In 1995, I fell down and hit my head on a concrete step and lost all of my memory. I am now beginning to get parts of my memory back. It is amazing that my son is an amnesia specialist. He has tried to help me. I have lost all my memory of God, but I am beginning to remember a few things about God. My husband tells me I used to teach Sunday School to children. I knew all the Bible stories but I couldn't remember any of them. Now I am beginning to get some of those back."

As she wept, she said, "You know I remember some aspect of the Holy Spirit and a little bit about Jesus. I do not understand or remember anything about God. I was wondering if you could help me to deal with this area of my life? I love Jesus, but I have no concept or memory of God."

I looked at her and said something to her that I was not sure at the time I should say. I said to her, "Why in the world would you be crying over something you have no concept of?"

She said, "I do not know."

I responded, "I do not believe that you have lost your memory of God. I believe you have blocked out your view of God because you are angry at Him for falling and hitting your head and losing your memory." Her husband was sitting in a place where only I could see him. He was shaking his head to indicate, "YES!" I said, "What you need to do is to get alone with God and ask Him to work out this stubborn spot in your life that you are not willing to give up to Him."

I later found out she was a photographer. That night at the service, she came back and brought a picture of the place in the prayer garden where God had changed her. She had driven to the city and had it enlarged and framed. I still have that picture. She wrote a note on the back of it for me.

She said, "When you shared with me that Jesus said, 'Put your hands on the plow and do not look backwards,' those words captured my attention. Deal with the stubborn spots in your life now, the ones that are in front of you, and go on with your life in Christ. I went to the prayer garden and spent time with the Lord and repented." She then said, "I want to give you this. It's a picture to help you know the spot where God changed my life. I love God with all my heart, soul, and mind and now I know who He is."

There are many confusing situations in life that do not make a lot of sense, but God is never confused about your life. He is never confused about the pressure that He is putting on your life or why He is doing it. You may continue asking questions like, "Why am I so restless? Why am I so anxious or nervous or unhappy? Why do I hurt? Why am I so disturbed? Why do I worry so much?"

Your success and your career may be going well; your achievement in school can be tremendous; the friends you have may be great; but if you are not submitting to the Hands of the Master and the pressure that He is putting on your life to bring great change, you will be asking those same questions for years. "God, my public life seems fine, but there is something within me that just does not seem right–what is it?"

When a potter could not get the clay to submit to the pressure, he would crush that clay vessel and start all over. He had a new vessel in mind. God can always work good in your life, but when you disobey Him you can never make up what could have been. When I was serving with Dr. Henry Blackaby, author of the study *Experiencing God*, he once said to me, "Kerry, can you imagine standing before God and God saying to you, 'Kerry, let me show you what could have been in your life if you had only obeyed me back there on that day.' "

It is critical that moment-by-moment and day-by-day we obey the Lord in everything that He brings to our lives. If a potter cannot remove the stubborn spot, he or she will remove that vessel in the marred shape, unfinished and deformed, walk out to the field and set it in the sun to harden. When it hardens, the potter will break it and never use it again.

Alison and I want to be used by our Master. We are sure you do too! We want the Lord to take us and mold us in the way He has in mind. Understand, God will only let you resist so long.

Burning Thought #4

And the vessel that he made of clay was marred in the hand of the potter; so he made it again into another vessel, as it seemed good to the potter to make.

Jeremiah 18:4

Focus on Christ

Can you be still long enough for God to shape you? Do you believe God has a better plan in mind for your life than you do? How would you know what God wants to shape you to become? These are questions everyone needs to ponder.

Have you ever tried to dress a squirming preschooler? It seems like an impossible task. The parent is interested in making the child presentable to match the occasion. There is just one problem. Children have much more on their mind than getting dressed! Staying still and co-operating is not a child's focus. Thinking of playing with a toy, going outside, or getting something to eat drives the child to activity.

Many times believers are like these preschoolers. They want to have fun but ignore what it takes to get prepared for life. Staying still is not on their agenda. They are looking for activity that increases their possessions, positions, and even their influence. Activity can be masked to look like activity for God when many times it is simply trying to find out what we can do to make God proud of our success.

God is the Potter and we are the clay. To be molded and shaped by the Master, we must be still and abide in His hands. Jesus said that without Him we could do nothing. Yet, many times we think we must do something! Shaping requires being still in the Hands of God and letting Him speak to us through His Word. There is no substitute for spending time with God. Having a good attitude, a positive thought life, or an encouraging word is not the same as sitting in the counsel of God and hearing what He wants to do with your life. When God gives you direction, it is like a fire in your soul that will not let you go. You cannot get your mind off of what God shapes in your soul. You want to go further in your relationship with Him when He gives you wisdom.

Focus on Self

To avoid being still, and letting God shape you into the vessel He wants, brings discouragement, worry, and tension to your life. It is impossible to feel good about yourself when you hinder the very thing God is wanting to do in your life. You might say that you are not resisting God when you avoid His Word. When you avoid spending time in His Word and miss out on His purpose–that is rebellion.

Chapter Five

God's Hand: Corrects and Teaches

And you have done worse than your fathers, for behold, each one follows the dictates of his own evil heart, so that no one listens to Me.

Jeremiah 16:12

Alison

I became a born again believer in 2006 at the age of 26. I was attending a *Community Bible Study*. One of the main attractions for me was that they had child-care, and I was really wanting some help with my one-year-old son. The Bible study would give me a chance for a break. While child-care drew me, it was there that I met Jesus, and my life changed forever.

As I think back on that time, I remember God showing me all the things from which He had delivered me. I hungered to learn more about Him. My family began attending church regularly, and I began pursuing the call that God had placed on my life for counseling. This was not a call that I received easily. I battled the idea of being a counselor and really wanted no part of it, but God continuously pointed me in that direction.

I finally surrendered and began attending a church that had a counseling program. Not long after that, I began pursuing a Master's Degree in Professional Counseling from a Christian University. I was like a sponge and wanted to learn as much as I could. I read so many books on counseling and attended counselor training provided by the church. A few years later I made it to the end of my Master's program. Then, I began my pursuit of a State License in Professional Counseling. I took my board exam and passed. Next, I had to obtain the required hours of supervised practicum to receive this licensure. Then, things took a wrong turn. At least that is what I believed.

When I came to Christ at age 26, I had no Bible training at all. The truth of God's Word was not in me. I believed what I was taught through my education and did not recognize what was of God or what was of the world. Though I did attend a Christian university, the program that I learned under was an integration model. This model seeks to combine theology and psychology. At this point in my walk with God I believed that Christian meant biblical. While I did learn a tremendous amount of truth from my master's program, it was integrated with the world's ways. According to James 1:27, pure and undefiled religion is to keep oneself unspotted from the world.

I was stepping into the secular world of counseling with a heart full of God's ways and the world's ways and did not completely know the difference. This was a dangerous position. I started to be "like a wave of the sea driven and tossed by the wind" (James 1:6). I was tossed about for almost three years. Then, I found myself sitting in an auditorium in front of the State Licensing Board for a hearing of a complaint filed against me by my supervisor.

During the course of those three years my family had started attending the church where Kerry was the pastor, and I had started to learn from him. It is important to stress that Kerry's teaching was strictly from God's Word. The truths of the Bible had already started to convict my heart of the wrong ways in which I was going. The hearing with the board became a huge spiritual marker in my life. Through that, I turned to God. I was completely dependent on Him for help during that time. My heart was completely willing to yield to the direction that He would have me go. Had I not been receiving the teaching from God's Word, I may not have recognized what God was trying to show me. It has been quite a journey, but I can honestly say that the course correction came from the Word of God through the Holy Spirit.

About a year later during a Sunday service, Pastor Kerry, gave an altar call for twelve members to join a *MasterLife* group that he and

Elaine would be leading in their home. I accepted the call and began attending. This was the same teaching that enlightened Kerry's mind in 1981 and brought him to a deeper growth in Christ. What none of us knew at the time was that God would call Kerry and Elaine out of that church to move to Georgia only a few months into the teaching. When Kerry and Elaine moved, it was a very difficult time for me. I do not know what I would have done if God had not prepared me through the *MasterLife* teaching. I grew in my walk with God during that time taking me to a new depth of learning and trust. It is amazing that 36 years later, Kerry used that tool to teach me the things he had learned. *MasterLife* was written by a godly man, Avery Willis, who sat in the counsel of the Lord.

The Lord has brought Kerry and I together to teach others all that God has taught us. Our desire is not to teach our own words, or our own thinking. Our desire is to sit in the counsel of the Lord and share with others all that God is teaching us. Kerry's word is not like a fire. Alison's word is not like a fire. Only God's Word is like a fire. It is the only teaching that is profitable for the spiritual development of a Christian.

The Profit of Scripture

> *All Scripture is given by inspiration of God, and is profitable for doctrine, for reproof, for correction, for instruction in righteousness, that the man of God may be complete, thoroughly equipped for every good work.*
>
> **2 Timothy 3:16-17**

Do you believe that all Scripture is given by inspiration of God? We live in a day in which God's Word is being changed, added to, and discredited to fit the desires of man. This completely erodes away the exact intent of God's Word for helping to develop a maturing Christian. If you do not believe that God's Word is perfect as given, then the Word of God will not be alive in your life.

Not until I completely surrendered to the truth that God's Word is right and any single thing that comes against it is wrong, did my spiritual life begin to develop deeper. My own thoughts, emotions, and actions were being penetrated by God's Word. The most crucial part of spiritual development is learning to live in God's Word and apply it to daily living. The power of the Holy Spirit is provided to shape the believer into becoming more and more like Jesus Christ. When we accept that all Scripture is given by inspiration of God, we can then learn how the Word of God is profitable, beneficial, and valuable to the Christian's life. Let's take a look at how God took me from a rebellious enemy to a completely surrendered follower of Jesus.

Doctrine:

For our purpose of understanding doctrine, think of it as simply the Scripture we use for teaching the faith. *Doctrine is our set of beliefs from the Bible that guide our thoughts, life, and teaching.*

By the time I began attending church with Kerry as my pastor, I had started to learn more of the Bible. I had been reading my Bible every day, but I began to realize that too much of my reading consisted of man's interpretation. I needed more reading of pure Scripture. When I began attending Sunday School and digging into God's Word, I began to learn more and more about the faith of a Christian. The teaching that I was receiving from the Word of God was deepening my relationship with Him. You cannot grow spiritually without the teaching of the faith. When we are not profiting or gaining insight from Scripture, we will be anemic in what we believe about God.

God's Word teaches us about God. How simple is that? As I grew in understanding of who God was, I began to see the areas of my life that needed to be cleaned up. God's church is crucial for the spiritual growth of a Christian. The local church was designed by God to be a place where we receive teaching. How do we know if we are walking in the ways of the world versus the ways of God if we do not have solid teaching from God's Word? How would you know if the world has seeped into your thinking, your workplace, your family, or your education? God's Word will reprove your thinking.

Reproof

Once again, we will keep our concept of reproof simple. *Reproof means to use Scripture for the purpose of correcting error.*

One of the areas in which I was still engaging in the world was drinking alcoholic beverages. I grew up in South Louisiana where drinking alcohol is a way of life. After receiving Christ at age 26, I did not stop drinking alcohol; nor had I felt convicted of drinking alcohol until one day when my daughter said, "Mom, drunkenness is a sin, and I think you need to stop drinking alcohol."

My response was what most responses are, "Well, Jesus turned water into wine, and it is discussed throughout the Bible. So, I am not convinced that drinking is a sin unless you drink to be drunk." In that moment, God used my little girl as a means of reproof! I could not get away from what she said!

It became my mission to search the Scripture to find a Word that would prove my believed truth on alcohol. This is a wonderful way for someone to find the truth. Get them in God's Word. As I began searching, God began speaking to me through His Word. The first Word that cut my heart was:

> *And do not be drunk with wine, in which is dissipation; but be filled with the Spirit*

Ephesians 5:18

As I read that Scripture, the conviction that came upon my heart made me ask the questions, "Do I love alcohol more than God? Why am I fighting this so much?" I just could not get away from the Word. I want to be clear here. I did not drink alcohol every day, nor was it necessary for me to function. I would hang out with friends on weekends and get drunk. As I continued that battle with God and His Word, it started to become more evident to me that when I would drink I would feel awful. Finally one day I was reading my Bible and read this:

> *It is good neither to eat meat nor drink wine nor do anything by which your brother stumbles or is offended or is made weak.*

Romans 14:21

This Scripture broke my heart. My desire for alcohol had the potential to cause a brother to stumble. In that moment, I realized that my witness to others of Jesus Christ was made void. I surrendered and deeply repented to the Lord. He heard my cry and completely cleansed me of all desire for alcohol. I have not had a drink of any kind of alcohol since that day of surrender. I have no desire for it. God removed the desire and replaced it with a deeper desire for Him. Now I can witness to everyone that God's Spirit is worth far more than any pleasurable moment of drinking. I do not regret giving up alcohol. It is a pivotal moment in my rapid spiritual growth in Christ. He brought me closer to Him. I am not revealing this to condemn others; but, if the Holy Spirit convicts our hearts of sin, and we do not obey God and surrender, we quench the Spirit and our spiritual development. It is extremely harmful to stop growing spiritually. God is not done developing me yet. He will not only reprove me, He will correct me.

Correction

What does the passage mean that Scripture is profitable for correction? *It means that Scripture is used to reset the direction of a person's life.*

When I review my life, it is difficult to believe the reset button that God has pushed in my life. At age 18 I became pregnant outside of marriage. Hannah was born nine months later. Hannah was seven years old when I came to know the Lord. Little did I know that she was watching me grow in Christ. When Hannah reached the tenth grade, I began to homeschool her. Many different reasons brought our family to this decision. At the time, I had no idea what that decision would do for the direction of my family's life.

The homeschool program we began using is called *Abeka*. This program is centered around the Word of God. At that time of her life, Hannah had been a horseback rider for close to ten years. We attended horse shows on weekends. Shortly after beginning homeschooling, Hannah came to me and said, "Mom, I do not want to ride horses on Sundays anymore. I want to honor the Lord's day and attend church."

I would love to say that I agreed but that was not the case. Why? Because I absolutely loved watching her ride at horse shows. I knew that without riding on Sundays she would have no chance of competition. She asked if we could go and talk about this with Pastor Kerry. I agreed. After church one Sunday, we went in Kerry's office, and Hannah shared her heart. In true pastor form, Kerry agreed that we must keep the Lord's day holy. As we completed our talk and began to leave the office, Kerry pulled me aside and said, "Don't you dare get in the way of the Holy Spirit's conviction on Hannah's heart." After that meeting, every time I opened my Bible, God was convicting me of the importance of keeping the Lord's day holy! I decided to heed the advice, and Hannah stopped showing horses on Sundays.

There was still one issue. My son Parker played in baseball tournaments which included playing on Sundays. I pulled Parker aside and told him that God had convicted my heart that we were to keep the Lord's day holy and that I was going to stop attending his games on Sundays. He said, "I understand Mom. I want you to do that." Thinking back about that situation I realized that I never told him not to play baseball on Sunday.

When Parker reached the seventh grade, my husband and I decided to start homeschooling him. We loved the fact that *Abeka* was Christ-centered. One day Parker came downstairs and said, "Mom, I don't want to play baseball on Sunday anymore. I was in history class and read this verse: "Remember the Sabbath day, to keep it holy" (Exodus 20:8).

I agreed with his desire and supported him. I told him that we would talk to his dad. Parker was a very good baseball player, and his team and coach were unwilling to let him go easily. I watched my twelve-year-old son stand up for his faith stronger and more courageous than I see many grown men do today. After Parker stood up for the conviction from the Holy Spirit, his desire for the Lord excelled. He began spending time with God daily even though I never told him to. God blessed him with a love for His Word. Next, we found a homeschool baseball team that did not play on Sunday.

About the same time that all this was happening, I was attending a Bible study. While completing my homework for the week, I came across this verse:

> *If you turn away your foot from the Sabbath, from doing your pleasure on My holy day, and call the Sabbath a delight, the holy day of the LORD honorable, and shall honor Him, not doing your own ways, nor finding your own pleasure, nor speaking your own words, then you shall delight yourself in the LORD; and I will cause you to ride on the high hills of the earth, and feed you with the heritage of Jacob your father. The mouth of the LORD has spoken.*

Isaiah 58:13-14

I realized that Parker was delighting in the Lord because he was obedient to the command placed on his heart. When he did, God blessed his obedience. Parker is now fourteen and has since shared that he believes God has called him to be a pastor.

God's Word reset my entire family's course of life. By allowing God to become first place in our lives, He created a generational shift toward holiness. The profit of Scripture guides the believer to line up his or her life with the truth of God's Word. God is a Holy God. In order to grow in a deeper relationship with Him, He molds the heart to be more like Him–Holy. If we are not interested in holiness then we are not interested in God. I can honestly say that I am watching my children love the Lord with all their hearts. Every morning Parker comes into my room and we discuss what God is teaching him. Hannah is in college but often we text and talk about Scripture and the Lord. This blows me away. God has taken our family and set us on a whole new path of life. How? By the leadership of His Holy Spirit and His Word. We read His Word, His Holy Spirit convicts, and we obey. Obedience to God's Word brings blessings that are far greater than anything the world has to offer. Once corrected, then we need instruction for right living.

Instruction in Righteousness

What does the passage mean that Scripture is profitable for instruction in righteousness? *It means that Scripture can be used to train a person in right and good living.*

Training implies practice and practice implies effort. Most Christians desire to do something that looks like work for the Lord, but few desire to put forth the effort required to have an intimate relationship with Him. My daughter Hannah went through many difficult times when she was learning horseback riding. She fell off a horse more times than I could count! But she was determined to always get back on and continue learning. I was her biggest critic, until I decided to take up horseback riding lessons. I realized quickly that when you watch someone ride a horse you do not understand what they are experiencing. You have to accomplish the task of riding a horse to gain understanding. I gained respect for my daughter as I watched what she was able to accomplish on the back of a horse.

She trained for ten years! Toward the end of her horseback riding days she was jumping 4 foot jumps and loving every minute of it. One thing that stuck out to me was that she always did much better on the horses with which she had a real connection. We did not have much money for training. We had to do all of our own work with our horses. The good thing about that is that it meant we had to spend a great amount of time with them. This created a relationship and a bond which in turn created trust. Trust is not something that is automatic with horses. It requires spending time with and learning about the horse. This is true for our relationship with God. Training in righteousness requires trusting God. Christians are not born trusting God.

Developing a "trusting God characteristic" is acquired by spending time with Him and learning about Him in a personal relationship. Jesus is our righteousness! In order to be trained in righteous living we must learn and practice His Ways. When we enter into the ways of the kingdom of God, it requires a different kind of life. This life requires holiness, not sinfulness. In order to learn this new way of life, we must be trained in the area of holiness. That means to learn the ways of righteous living.

Instruction in right living is a lifelong education that requires dependency on the One we love. Developing this love requires God to be placed in His proper place in our lives. The world has no place in the development of a Christian.

Quick to Listen

God's Word is like a fire to the life of His child. A person in right relationship with Him will quickly listen to and obey His Word. Scripture is of no profit to the one who pays no attention to what it says. Conviction is the work of the Holy Spirit. The Holy Spirit reveals to the believer the area of life that does not line up with God's Word. When the believer does not listen to the convicting power of the Holy Spirt, it is only a matter of time before he or she is in the dilemma described in the book of Jeremiah. God said to them, "Each one follows the dictates of his own evil heart, so that no one listens to Me" (Jeremiah 16:12). Then He said,

"The heart is deceitful above all things, and desperately wicked; who can know it?

Jeremiah 17:9

God is the only One who knows the deceit in the heart of a believer. He reveals this deceit by His Word to the one who is seeking Him. Why? In order to cleanse and remove the deceit that keeps His child in bondage. This removal requires hearing God's Word, receiving it, and accepting what He is saying. How do you hear the Word of God? Jesus discussed the types of hearers in a parable.

Then He spoke many things to them in parables, saying: "Behold, a sower went out to sow. And as he sowed, some seed fell by the wayside; and the birds came and devoured them. Some fell on stony places, where they did not have much earth; and they immediately sprang up because they had no depth of earth. But when the sun was up they were scorched, and because they had no root they withered away. And some fell among thorns, and the thorns sprang up and choked them. But others fell on good ground and yielded a crop: some a hundredfold, some sixty, some thirty. He who has ears to hear, let him hear!"

Matthew 13:3-9

After Jesus spoke this parable to the crowd, the disciples came and said to Him,

"Why do You speak to them in parables?"

He answered and said to them, "Because it has been given to you to know the mysteries of the kingdom of heaven, but to them it has not been given.

Matthew 13:10-11

God granted the disciples the ability to know the mysteries of the kingdom of heaven. God continues today to provide the mysteries of the kingdom to those that walk with Him. Through the power of the Holy Spirit, God grants understanding to the believer who hears His Words and obeys His Voice. Do you believe that? Jesus said to the disciples:

For whoever has, to him more will be given, and he will have abundance; but whoever does not have, even what he has will be taken away from him. Therefore I speak to them in parables, because seeing they do not see, and hearing they do not hear, nor do they understand.

Matthew 13:12-13

As a believer in Christ, the keys to the kingdom are available to the one who will walk with God. To him or her who has, more will be given, and he or she will have abundance. Abundance from God! By hearing God's Word and surrendering to His Ways, all that is available in the treasury of God is available to the one who loves Him. It is it difficult to hear that things we are currently practicing are sinful. Yet, once received and accepted, it is revealed just how small a believer's thinking can be. To believe that those things of the world are better than the abundance that God provides is small thinking. Do you desire for God to give you the mysteries of the kingdom? If so, then ask yourself, "How do I hear the Word of God?"

Look at Jesus' explanation to the disciples of the parable of the sower. *First*, Jesus shows how the hearer had an *unresponsive* heart.

"Therefore hear the parable of the sower: When anyone hears the word of the kingdom, and does not understand it, then the wicked one comes and snatches away what was sown in his heart. This is he who received seed by the wayside.

Matthew 13:18-19

He hears the Word but is not prepared to receive nor understand it. The ground between the tilled soil is hard packed from the farmer walking up and down the row. When a seed falls on these places, the soil is not receptive to it and it stays on the surface. This unresponsive hearer would be like a person who heard the truth but said, "I hear what they are saying, but I am not going to listen and change."

Second, Jesus explains that the next hearer is a *spontaneous* hearer.

But he who received the seed on stony places, this is he who hears the word and immediately receives it with joy; yet he has no root in himself, but endures only for a while. For when tribulation or persecution arises because of the word, immediately he stumbles.

Matthew 13:20-21

He received the Word temporarily but did not let it take root in the heart. It would be like a person hearing a wonderful sermon or teaching and saying, "Wasn't that a wonderful truth!" But then, a little trouble happens and they say, "God doesn't love me!"

Third, Jesus revealed a *distracted* hearer. He receives the Word, but lets the worries of this world and desire for things choke it out.

> *Now he who received seed among the thorns is he who hears the word, and the cares of this world and the deceitfulness of riches choke the word, and he becomes unfruitful.*
> **Matthew 13:22**

The worries of the world or the thoughts of great wealth distract this hearer from the thoughts and truths of God's Word. The poor person may be consumed with thinking, "If only I were rich, I would be happy." The wealthy person may be thinking, "If only I had more riches, I would be satisfied." Neither of these distracted hearers can be blessed or be a blessing.

Lastly, Jesus says there is a *responsive* hearer. He receives the Word, understands it, bears fruit, and brings forth results.

> *But he who received seed on the good ground is he who hears the word and understands it, who indeed bears fruit and produces: some a hundredfold, some sixty, some thirty.*
> **Matthew 13:23**

The difference is the degree of fruitfulness. All receive the Word, but some put it to use more than others and have a greater yield.

What type of hearer are you? Are there things in your life that you place above God and His Word? If so you will not receive the mysteries of the kingdom. Anything that has a Christian's affections other than God has the ability to move them away from the truth. Alison had to accept that alcohol and the pleasure of life had her affection over the Lord. Once she accepted this truth, she was able to do what the Word instructed and repent of her sin. The Lord then removed her desire for alcohol and replaced it with a deeper love for Him.

God did the same thing for Alison's children. Once they heard from God and accepted the truth, they were willing to obey His Voice. This obedience led to a greater understanding of the mysteries of the kingdom. *Responsive* hearers hear God's Word and do what He says.

But be doers of the word, and not hearers only, deceiving yourselves.

James 1:22

Before a Christian can become a doer of God's Word, they must become a hearer that has a desire to line his or her life up with the truth. There is a lot at stake for a believer who decides that they are not interested in walking in the Ways of the Lord, "even what he has will be taken away from him" (Matthew 13:12). Not listening to God and heeding His instruction produces deception in the heart. The danger results in the believer being blind to the deception and therefore left in peril.

God's desire for His children does not end at salvation. His desire for His children begins at salvation. He has riches beyond our imagination and waits to bless the ones who love Him. The problem comes when His children will not listen to Him. God's Hand corrects and teaches for the purpose of a deeper relationship with Him. Allow Him to correct and teach you. You will never regret anything that is a gift from your Heavenly Father.

Burning Thought #5

And you have done worse than your fathers, for behold, each one follows the dictates of his own evil heart, so that no one listens to Me.

Jeremiah 16:12

Focus on Christ

Though we can do what we want, our ways are not hidden from the Lord! What does it mean to follow the dictates of your own heart? In this passage the emphasis is on a people who are following their wrong, evil hearts. That means that they follow a twisted imagination, way, or lust instead of following after the Words of God.

God was placing His Hand on His people because they had gone after their own thinking, desires, lusts, and imaginations. Their heart had turned from God! His response–strong discipline. Does that seem harsh to you? It shouldn't. God brings discipline to correct, teach, and bring His children back to a deep relationship with Him.

I hear many people say, "As long as I am not hurting anyone else, it is okay for me to do what I want." But, in the body of Christ, you cannot sin independently of others. We are all in one body–the body of Christ. When one part hurts, the whole body feels the sensation.

Others say, "Well, here is what I think!" That does not get God's attention! He is not interested in what we think; He is interested in us learning to walk in the ways of His holiness. Doing what is right in your own eyes is not the same as doing what God says in His Word.

Our tendency is to follow our heart. Be careful though because our heart can convince us something that is wrong seems right. The desires of your heart are fine to follow when you are abiding in Christ, His Word, and His Ways. But when you are discouraged, in despair, anxious, or confused, it is not a time to follow your heart.

Notice the key thought at the end of this verse: "So that no one listens to Me." There is the problem. If they listen to God, then direction would be right. In order to hear someone, you must be close enough to know what they are saying. God's Word helps you measure whether your ways are right or wrong.

Focus on Self

To focus on self is simple. Give in to your own desires, thoughts, and wants. Ignore God's Word for a couple of days, or hours, and you will be back to your old way of thinking. But Christ came into your life and made you a new creation. This new being He made requires a new diet. You cannot feed on twisted imaginations and desires and experience this new life. God's Word is the wonderful new diet that will guide your life from selfishness to service.

Chapter Six

God's Hand: Fearful to Faithful

"Blessed is the man who trusts in the LORD, and whose hope is the LORD. For he shall be like a tree planted by the waters, which spreads out its roots by the river, and will not fear when heat comes; but its leaf will be green, and will not be anxious in the year of drought, nor will cease from yielding fruit.
Jeremiah 17:7-8

Alison

Have you ever been afraid? If you are a living human being, there has most likely been a time in your life when you have been afraid. What is strange to think about is that when I recall the events of the house fire, fear was not something I was thinking about or could identify. In fact, after my mom and I returned home from the hospital, I can honestly say that I did not have any fear or nightmares from the memories of the fire. My mom did have a fear of closing her bedroom door. She slept with the door open for a long time. Thinking back on this, I recognize that I did not have much understanding of what had happened to us in the fire. I did not recognize the power of the fire and how we were so close to death.

Our Response

As humans, we cannot know how we will respond in the presence of danger. It challenges our thinking to consider how we would react in the face of death. The truth is that while we consider and process how we would respond to a crisis, we do not know how we will respond until that moment arrives. God knows exactly how we will respond because He knows all things. If God told you how you would respond in the presence of danger, would you believe Him? This exact situation happened to Simon Peter. Jesus spoke to His disciples and said,

> *"All of you will be made to stumble because of Me this night, for it is written: 'I will strike the Shepherd, and the sheep of the flock will be scattered.' But after I have been raised, I will go before you to Galilee."*
>
> **Matthew 26:31-32**

Then Peter responded,

> *"Even if all are made to stumble because of You, I will never be made to stumble."*
>
> **Matthew 26:33**

Jesus shocked Peter by what He said next,

> *"Assuredly, I say to you that this night, before the rooster crows, you will deny Me three times."*
>
> **Matthew 26:34**

Peter could never imagine that he would deny Christ, much less do it three times! So Peter tried to help Christ see that He was wrong.

> *"Even if I have to die with You, I will not deny You!" And so said all the disciples.*
>
> **Matthew 26:35**

In this account of Peter's interaction, Jesus shared with the disciples from Zechariah 13:7, "Strike the Shepherd, and the sheep will be scattered." He was letting them know exactly what would happen and used the Word of God to confirm it. Peter responded that he would never be made to stumble. It became clear that Peter did not recognize that Jesus knew exactly how everyone would respond. Have you ever heard a Word from God but thought you knew better than Him?

It is critical to understand that Peter was not a stranger to Jesus. He was a disciple chosen by Jesus.

> *And Jesus, walking by the Sea of Galilee, saw two brothers, Simon called Peter, and Andrew his brother, casting a net into the sea; for they were fishermen. Then He said to them, "Follow Me, and I will make you fishers of men." They immediately left their nets and followed Him.*
>
> **Matthew 4:18-20**

Peter left his net and followed Jesus immediately. Jesus knew everything that would take place until the end of Peter's life. Peter would be wise to learn from the Son of God! Up to this point in Peter's life, every relationship that he had was a human-to-human relationship. He needed to learn how to adjust to a relationship with Jesus. This kind of relationship would require submission to His authority. Peter thought he knew the truth about himself. He believed because he loved Jesus, that he would never deny Him. Jesus knew him better. He knew what Peter would do, and He knew what was at stake.

The relationship between Peter and Jesus is recorded throughout the Gospel accounts. It is clear that Peter did love Jesus, so what happened when he denied Him three times? Simon Peter denied Jesus because of fear. Immediately afterward, he remembered Jesus' Words and wept bitterly. Peter was right in the midst of the activity of God who would provide salvation to the world, and yet he was so afraid. Similar to how I did not recognize the power of fire, Peter did not recognize the power of his God. Courage comes when you have a high confidence in self, which causes you to be blind to the danger of a situation. There is no fear when you do not see the danger. The opposite would happen if you had low confidence in self. This would produce crippling fear. But, confidence in God produces faith, a healthy fear of Him, and a right view of the situation.

Jesus knew how Peter would respond and still chose him as a disciple. Have you ever received a Word from God yet thought you knew better? Imagine sitting with the Word of God–Jesus, hearing straight from His mouth, and still believing you knew better. God always knows what He is doing. He knew that when He selected this simple fisherman Peter would ultimately become a co-laborer of Jesus Christ. He also knew there was much work to do in the spiritual growth of Simon Peter.

When we are called to a relationship with Christ, we are not immediately developed as a co-laborer with Jesus. Much like the physical development of a child, Peter needed to grow and develop spiritually. Do you recall the five spiritual development stages that were introduced in Chapter 1? Below is a recap of those phases. As you read, notice how Peter developed under the training of Christ. Most of the time we see the weakness of Peter, but it was still an opportunity given to him by Jesus to begin development as a strong leader. With these phases in mind, let's take a look at the journey of Peter and the role Jesus played in guiding his development.

Unbeliever

This first stage shows that our role as a believer is to be a witness and our task is evangelism. That means that in this stage the unbeliever has very little responsibility. As believers, we must start the flame of growth by being a friend to the unbeliever and looking for the opportunity to present Christ.

One of the two who heard John speak and followed Him was Andrew, Simon Peter's brother. Andrew immediately found his brother, Simon, and said to him, "We have found the Messiah" (which is translated, the Christ) and brought him to Jesus.

> *Now when Jesus looked at him, He said, "You are Simon the son of Jonah. You shall be called Cephas" (which is translated, A Stone).*
> **John 1:40-42**

In this account, Andrew, Peter's brother, shares about Christ and takes him to meet Jesus. When Peter is introduced to Jesus, He knows exactly who he is and exactly His purpose. Now Jesus becomes Peter's spiritual guide in development.

Spiritual Babe

In this second phase, an unbeliever has just received Christ and is now a spiritual babe. If we do not help the babe, he or she will never grow. Our role to the babe is to be a parent and our task is to help him or her develop. If the fire of God's Word is to flame up in the spiritual babe's life, some help is needed. We cannot force growth, but we can provide help when one is receptive to growth. The spiritual babe is watching and observing, not necessarily trying to do what Jesus is doing. Peter watched as Jesus did His work.

> *Now when Jesus had come into Peter's house, He saw his wife's mother lying sick with a fever. So He touched her hand, and the fever left her. And she arose and served them.*
> **Matthew 8:14-15**

While He spoke these things to them, behold, a ruler came and worshiped Him, saying, "My daughter has just died, but come and lay Your hand on her and she will live." So Jesus arose and followed him, and so did His disciples. ....When Jesus came into the ruler's house, and saw the flute players and the noisy crowd wailing, He said to them, "Make room, for the girl is not dead, but sleeping." And they ridiculed Him. But when the crowd was put outside, He went in and took her by the hand, and the girl arose. And the report of this went out into all that land.

Matthew 9:18-19, 23-26

Spiritual Disciple

In this third phase, our role is to be a servant to the disciple and our task is that of a trainer. God causes the growth, but we help cultivate the person by teaching them how to get into God's Word. Many times they will fail. But, failure pushes the believer to place their faith in Christ.

Jesus came walking on the water toward the disciples who were in a boat. He was about to test and train Peter with a storm.

Now in the fourth watch of the night Jesus went to them, walking on the sea.

And Peter said, "Lord, if it is You, command me to come to You on the water."

So He said, "Come." And when Peter had come down out of the boat, he walked on the water to go to Jesus. But when he saw that the wind was boisterous, he was afraid; and beginning to sink he cried out, saying, "Lord, save me!"

And immediately Jesus stretched out His hand and caught him, and said to him, "O you of little faith, why did you doubt?" And when they got into the boat, the wind ceased.

Matthew 14:25-32

Another time, Jesus asked a probing question to Peter,

He said to them, "But who do you say that I am?"

Simon Peter answered and said, "You are the Christ, the Son of the living God."

Matthew 16:15-16

Peter answered correctly. He knew Jesus was much more than one of the other disciples.

Jesus taught the disciples that He must die and be raised again. But Peter had a human reaction. Though Peter was in training to become a spiritual disciple, he had not yet grown to where he needed to be.

> *Then Peter took Him aside and began to rebuke Him, saying, "Far be it from You, Lord; this shall not happen to You!"*
>
> *But He turned and said to Peter, "Get behind Me, Satan! You are an offense to Me, for you are not mindful of the things of God, but the things of men."*

Matthew 16:22-23

Progressing to deeper training, Jesus took Peter, James, and John up on the mountain and was transfigured before them. That must have been an incredible shock! But can you imagine the fear that came when they heard a voice from heaven?

> *...and suddenly a voice came out of the cloud, saying, "This is My beloved Son, in whom I am well pleased. Hear Him!" And when the disciples heard it, they fell on their faces and were greatly afraid.*

Matthew 17:5-6

Peter continued to be challenged by his own worldly ways and thinking. Jesus knew what Peter would become and continued to test and train him in the ways of God. Peter was bold and made statements many times that he could not live up to. Remember when he said,

> *Peter answered and said to Him, "Even if all are made to stumble because of You, I will never be made to stumble."*
>
> *Jesus said to him, "Assuredly, I say to you that this night, before the rooster crows, you will deny Me three times."*
>
> *Peter said to Him, "Even if I have to die with You, I will not deny You!" And so said all the disciples.*

Matthew 26:33-35

Can a spiritual disciple ever learn to be consistent? The answer is yes, but he or she must realize that every day is not a perfect spiritual high. There are days when physical and mental exhaustion is real. Peter and the disciples showed this when Jesus asked them to sit while He went to pray. Jesus poured His soul out to His Heavenly Father. When He finished praying, He came back to the disciples. The Scriptures reveal what He found.

> *Then He came to the disciples and found them sleeping, and said to Peter, "What! Could you not watch with Me one hour?*
>
> **Matthew 26:40**

If your close friend is challenged by someone in your presence, you will defend that friend. Peter did that with Jesus, but his way was wrong.

> *Then they came and laid hands on Jesus and took Him. And suddenly, one of those who were with Jesus stretched out his hand and drew his sword, struck the servant of the high priest, and cut off his ear.*
>
> **Matthew 26:51**

Though Peter would become one of the greatest leaders of the New Testament church, he failed when his life was at stake. What Jesus had said Peter would do, he did–he denied he knew Jesus!

> *Now Peter sat outside in the courtyard. And a servant girl came to him, saying, "You also were with Jesus of Galilee." But he denied it before them all, saying, "I do not know what you are saying."*
>
> *And when he had gone out to the gateway, another girl saw him and said to those who were there, "This fellow also was with Jesus of Nazareth."*
>
> *But again he denied with an oath, "I do not know the Man!"*
>
> *And a little later those who stood by came up and said to Peter, "Surely you also are one of them, for your speech betrays you."*
>
> *Then he began to curse and swear, saying, "I do not know the Man!" Immediately a rooster crowed. And Peter remembered the word of Jesus who had said to him, "Before the rooster crows, you will deny Me three times." So he went out and wept bitterly.*
>
> **Matthew 26:69-75**

When a Christian gives in to peer pressure for fear of being shunned by others, there is usually a wrong response. Some curse as Peter did, others drink, some tell dirty jokes, or they join in on some other fleshly desire, just so family or friends will not reject them.

The good news is that the story does not end here for Peter. God does not leave him in sorrow and despair. Peter's sorrow led to deep repentance and a deepening of faith in God. We witness the transformation in the book of Acts. First the promise of the Holy Spirit is fulfilled:

> *Then there appeared to them divided tongues, as of fire, and one sat upon each of them. And they were all filled with the Holy Spirit and began to speak with other tongues, as the Spirit gave them utterance.*
>
> **Acts 2:3-4**

Shortly after receiving the Spirit the same Peter who denied Christ gave a sermon witnessing to all the things that Jesus taught him.

> *"Therefore let all the house of Israel know assuredly that God has made this Jesus, whom you crucified, both Lord and Christ."*
>
> *Now when they heard this, they were cut to the heart, and said to Peter and the rest of the apostles, "Men and brethren, what shall we do?"*
>
> *Then Peter said to them, "Repent, and let every one of you be baptized in the name of Jesus Christ for the remission of sins; and you shall receive the gift of the Holy Spirit.*
>
> **Acts 2:36-38**

Only the Word of God can cut to the heart of a person. This is the exact message that Jeremiah shared from God to the false prophets in his day:

> *"Is not My word like a fire?" says the LORD, "And like a hammer that breaks the rock in pieces?*
>
> **Jeremiah 23:29**

Just as the prophets in Jeremiah's day believed that they knew better than God, so did Peter. When Jesus told Peter exactly what would happen, he boasted about how he would never deny him. But, there is a difference between the Old Testament false prophets and Peter. Peter was deeply convicted of his sin; the false prophets were not.

This deep change in Peter is evident as we witness him in the book of Acts. His preaching placed the name of Jesus on display and the words cut to the heart of the people. Peter spoke with authority! He stood in the counsel of God and knew the words to speak on His behalf.

Peter's fear had been a symptom of his unbelief. Just as I did not realize the power of the fire, Peter did not realize the power of his God. What do you believe about God? The way in which you respond in the face of danger and death is directly related to what you believe about God. Jesus knew Peter would deny Him, but Peter did not believe him.

Multiplying Leader

In this fourth phase, our role is that of a manager whose task is to equip the leader. It is important that the person not only stay in God's Word, but also continue to grow in God's Word. As the person grows in knowledge of and obedience to God's Word, he or she becomes a multiplying leader.

We do not see a great picture of Peter being a multiplying leader until after his deep repentance. Once that happened, God used him in an awesome way to develop the New Testament church and its leaders.

Peter–A Man of God

In reading these accounts of Peter's encounters with Jesus, it is clear and evident that Jesus had a purpose and a heavenly understanding for His relationship with Peter. He knew beforehand all that Peter would endure. His goal was to prepare Peter for the task. It was clear on several occasions that Peter did not understand the gravity of what was taking place. There were several occasions in which Peter responded from his flesh. Nothing, however, was so deep as when he denied Christ. This denial brought deep, godly sorrow to Peter's heart and mind. Why? Because his denial was the first offense toward his personal relationship with Jesus. He denied the One whom he loved.

Peter was a man with a courageous spirit. He was on the frontline with Jesus. He stood up and spoke and on a few occasions misspoke. Fear can make even the most courageous people say things that they will later regret. There will be times in your walk with God when you will have to either show courage or break and run. It is easy to tell people to believe God and move forward in their lives, but it is not as easy when the situation is personal. After this encounter, Peter was very disturbed. As you view all of the scriptural accounts of fear that Peter dealt with, it is interesting that each encounter was personal to him.

In order to develop, we must experience spiritual encounters with Jesus that will take us from witnessing what He can do for others, to experiencing Him personally for our lives. This requires encounters that may produce fear or faith. The answer to the fear in our walk with God lies in continual development of trusting God with our very life. The book of Jeremiah states:

"Blessed is the man who trusts in the LORD, and whose hope is the LORD. For he shall be like a tree planted by the waters, which spreads out its roots by the river, and will not fear when heat comes; but its leaf will be green, and will not be anxious in the year of drought, nor will cease from yielding fruit.

Jeremiah 17:7-8

Let's take one last look at the book of Mark to witness what happens when we do not trust in the power of God.

On the same day, when evening had come, He said to them, "Let us cross over to the other side." Now when they had left the multitude, they took Him along in the boat as He was. And other little boats were also with Him. And a great windstorm arose, and the waves beat into the boat, so that it was already filling. But He was in the stern, asleep on a pillow. And they awoke Him and said to Him, "Teacher, do You not care that we are perishing?"

Then He arose and rebuked the wind, and said to the sea, "Peace, be still!" And the wind ceased and there was a great calm. But He said to them, "Why are you so fearful? How is it that you have no faith?" And they feared exceedingly, and said to one another, "Who can this be, that even the wind and the sea obey Him!"

Mark 4:35-41

Here is another account of complete fear. In the midst of a storm, Truth (Jesus) is physically asleep in the boat. There are many things you can repair if you have the right skills, but man has yet to learn how to calm the weather. Jesus not only stopped the storm, but He also calmed the wind and the waves. Would that impress you? Yet, as Christians, we often doubt in God's ability to calm storms. How do I raise this child? How do I help my marriage? How do we make the finances work? It will take a big time God to fix these things. This same God who calmed the storm knew every detail of Peter's life before it ever happened. Is fear the problem, or unbelief? There is no fear in following God, just fear in trying to find your own way. Jesus has the real truth of the situation that you may fear. The question is, will you believe Him?

Kerry

I experienced several times in my life in which I had to lean on my faith in God. Here is one time that God showed up in a big way.

A few years after Elaine and I had moved to Campbellsville, Kentucky to attend college, we encountered a great need in our lives.

I surrendered to the call of God on my life to go into full-time Christian ministry. I really did not know what all that meant, but I knew it was God's plan for my life. One of the many things God taught us was how to depend on Him for everything in life.

I remember one Saturday night, I stayed up late to study and pray. Elaine and Jason were in bed, and I was sitting at my desk trying to focus. My attention was on a great need. We only had one can of food in the house, we had depleted our son's little piggy bank to make sure he had some food, and we had no money in the bank! What was I to do? I needed to take care of my family and was doing everything I knew possible to provide for us.

Elaine was a secretary for the registrar at the college. I was trying to bring in money by serving in several different ways. I worked part-time at the college by managing the print shop. My English professor owned a large home that was always needing remodeling or things moved, so I worked for him as often as possible. Late nights, I had a job of cleaning the large office complex for the Kentucky Division of Forestry, and also I served as music and youth director for Bradfordsville Baptist Church. All of this was going on while taking a full load of courses. That year, with all those sources of income, we only made a little over $4,000.

Troubled in my spirit with this information stirring in my mind, I got out of my chair from behind the desk and got on my knees to pray. As I wept, I said, "God, You sent us here to prepare for ministry. I am doing everything I know to do to provide for my family and pay for my education and living expenses. You said You would take care of us. We have no food to carry us through the next week. God, I must have money in the mail on Monday morning!"

While I was praying, I knew God could provide. But then, doubts began to fill my thoughts when I finished praying. Since going off to college, no one had tried to help us with expenses. Many others from our church had gone into ministry and would receive some kind of support, but that had not happened with us. No one was sending us money! Then I thought, "What am I thinking? This is Saturday night. The mail system has already run and they don't work on the weekend. We will never get money by Monday morning."

God then reminded me that He sent us there and would take care of our needs. We went to church on Sunday morning with prayerful hearts and hungry stomachs. We didn't tell anyone that we had need of food. When we arrived at church, several families came up to us and told us they had some groceries for us and wanted to put them in our car. God provided!

On Monday morning I rushed to the mailbox at the college to check and see if a miracle had happened. It had! I received two checks. One from my grandparents and the other from Elaine's aunt. Both had never given us anything in our life! As I raced back down the hill to the house, I praised God for His provision.

When God changes your unbelief into belief you forget your fears of having nothing and learn to live by faith. That experience was like a fire burning within me that never let me forget how God provides. It is more exciting to see Him provide than to never have a need to trust Him.

Co-Laborer

In this last phase, the fire of God's Word is burning to the hottest point and the person is now a co-laborer with the trainer. Our role in helping this person is to be an encourager and our task is to give support as he or she continues to develop in the way God has designed. But remember, God is the one who is the developer, we are just the encouragers. Peter became a co-laborer with Christ and with other key leaders. He had become a man who could be depended on to stay strong in the faith. He eventually was martyred for his deep faith.

There is no short cut in the progression from fear to faith. God has created one Way to Him. The process requires a willingness to yield to the Hand of God in order to allow Him to develop you into a person of faith. Only then will you trust Him through the storms of life. Are you willing to listen to the Lord? Are you willing to allow Christ to rebuke you, teach you, and train you as He did with Peter? And ultimately, are you willing to recognize when you are wrong and repent and return to fellowship with the Lord? Becoming a spiritual co-laborer requires all of these things. The desire stems from the fire of a deep burning love for the One who gave His life for us, Jesus.

Burning Thought #6

"Blessed is the man who trusts in the LORD, and whose hope is the LORD. For he shall be like a tree planted by the waters, which spreads out its roots by the river, and will not fear when heat comes; but its leaf will be green, and will not be anxious in the year of drought, nor will cease from yielding fruit.
Jeremiah 17:7-8

Focus on Christ

Do you want to be blessed? I think we all desire the blessings of God. But there is a connection between blessings and walking with Christ. If you want to be blessed, you must extend out your roots toward Christ and drink from the living water that only He can provide. But how do you do that? You must make the effort to have a deep connection with Christ which comes by abiding in His Word. This is the person who will be blessed.

Trust is placing your faith in God. Fear comes when you depend on self! You cannot trust God as long as you believe you can provide better than He can. And it is impossible to please God without faith. Many are unwilling to trust God to provide in a way better than human effort. People like this, whose hope is not in the Lord, will have fear when the heat and drought comes.

A tree planted by water does not have any worries about heat. As long as there is water, the tree will flourish. If the water dries up, the tree may die. But, as long as there is water, even a drought will not cause the tree to stop bearing fruit. Christ is our nourishment. As long as you depend on Him, troubles may come but they will not stop you from bearing fruit. Christ is our Way, our Truth, and literally, our Life! If you choose to spend time with Him, then everything that is needed in life will be available to you.

Focus on Self

In Matthew 16:26, Jesus said, *"For what profit is it to a man if he gains the whole world, and loses his own soul? Or what will a man give in exchange for his soul?"* The sad truth is that people will choose comfort, money, a nice house, and a good job for the expense of their soul!

Why would someone exchange the abundant life for fleshly pleasures? Maybe they have never tasted the relationship that is available through the living water of Christ. Or maybe they have never learned the nourishment that is available when trusting in God. It is interesting that God stated through Jeremiah 17:5, *"Thus says the LORD: "Cursed is the man who trusts in man and makes flesh his strength, whose heart departs from the LORD."*

If your heart departs from God, then you will trust in yourself. Many times you may gain what self seeks, but if you do, you will miss out on what God could have provided.

Section Three

The Voice of God

Chapter Seven

God's Voice: Public or Private

Call to Me, and I will answer you, and show you great and mighty things, which you do not know.

Jeremiah 33:3

Close But No Connection

Does not God's Word burn like a fire in our hearts? When we are in close connection with God our hearts are tender to the Word. Our soul is purified by its cleansing power. There are times when we want to be so close to Jesus that our heart, mind, and souls burn within us. The Word becomes a purifying and cleansing experience that sets our mind on the right path. The Voice of God seems so loud when your spirit is in close connection to your Savior.

We are involved in many different kinds of relationships in life. We have relationships with our family members, friends, co-workers, and classmates. Some of these relationships we choose and some we do not. The issue is not whether or not we have relationships, the issue is whether or not we have a connection with those in the relationship. It is safe to say that when we are at church for Sunday worship, we see many families that seem to have a connection. Would we see the same thing if we were to enter their home and view their life from the inside? What would we witness? Would we witness the same family in private that we do in public?

What we see in public is not always the same view that we see in private. Parents, do your children see the same mom and dad Monday through Saturday that they see on Sunday morning at church? Would your children want to serve the God you serve in private through the week? The dynamic of a family places the members of the family in a close physical environment. But being close physically is not the same as having a connection. In many marriages today, the husband and wife are in a relationship but there is a huge distance between them. They are close to one another in a physical space, but there is no connection. Marriages fail because they lack a connection. This kind of relationship destroys the whole fabric of our society because there is a physical closeness, but there is no real connection.

This was happening in Jesus' day. In learning about Peter's relationship with Jesus it is clear he was physically close to Him but at times he was not connected to the mind and heart of Christ. Peter spent much time physically with Christ, as did the other disciples. However, there were still many truths about the kingdom of God that the disciples did not understand.

In Mark 4:30-34 Jesus begins talking about the kingdom of God through a parable.

> Then He said, "To what shall we liken the kingdom of God? Or with what parable shall we picture it? It is like a mustard seed which, when it is sown on the ground, is smaller than all the seeds on earth; but when it is sown, it grows up and becomes greater than all herbs, and shoots out large branches, so that the birds of the air may nest under its shade."
>
> **Mark 4:30-32**

In order to make sense of the parable it is important to understand that a mustard seed was the smallest of seeds. When planted, it could grow to a very large size compared to its beginning. In fact, the mustard seed could grow into a plant that could house bird nests. It could grow to be 10-15 feet tall. However, keep in mind that Jesus is telling a parable. The major truth that He was describing was the kingdom of God and its small beginnings. The kingdom of God, though it began small, can develop into something quite large. Why did Jesus use parables?

And with many such parables He spoke the word to them as they were able to hear it.

Mark 4:33

According to the Scriptures, Jesus spoke in parables based upon what the people were able to hear. Not everyone is able to hear the truth in regard to the kingdom. Jesus told Peter that he would deny Him three times, but Peter was unable to hear Him. Jesus spoke in parables when He was sharing and teaching a group of people in public. He always knew what each person was able to hear. Jesus also knows each person's private life. He knew who had a desire to have a connection with Him and who did not.

Kerry

Many years ago, I was reading this same passage in Mark 4:30-34 during my daily time with God. He began to speak to me through this passage. As I was reading, He began to show me truth that I had never seen before. Jesus said that He used parables to speak to the people. Sometimes the deeper meaning was hidden from the public. But notice what Jesus did next.

But without a parable He did not speak to them. And when they were alone, He explained all things to His disciples.

Mark 4:34

He explained ALL things to His disciples. This took place when He was alone with them. And Jesus shared this truth with me when I was alone with Him. How much time do you spend alone with Jesus?

Jesus revealed the truth to those closest to Him. He explained that when He was in public He spoke in parables, but when He was in private He explained the depth of the parable to His disciples. God desires to share ALL truth to His disciples who spend time alone with Him. If you are faithful to be in His Word, He can share with you just as He shared with me the truth that was eye-opening and life-changing. He will share with you the truth of your heart and lead you into the way He would have you go. But understand many of these truths are shared in private. While you may be convicted by the Holy Spirit at church in a public setting and have a huge change, real lasting change continues as we spend time in private with Jesus. He desires to share the truths of the kingdom with a believer who will make a connection with Him.

During Jesus' day, the disciples were dealing with the Roman Empire. The Roman Empire was huge and the disciples knew the magnitude of it. Can you imagine what went through the minds of the twelve disciples? They were probably saying, "Jesus, You want us to do what, with only twelve?" Can you imagine the structure of the Jewish leaders composed of Scribes, Pharisees, and Sadducees–and that was just the religious structure? Then think of the whole Roman Empire. I am sure the disciples were thinking, "What is Jesus thinking? He is telling us the kingdom is like a mustard seed and we only have a little to work with." Can you imagine gathering some of your friends and saying, "I know the U.S. government is large, but there are five of us! Let's go change the structure in a few months." It would seem ridiculous.

Yet, in this passage, we see that the kingdom of God is being initiated by a small band of believers selected by Jesus. Jesus was teaching them what the kingdom of God looks like in its beginnings. He was speaking to this small group who would begin the kingdom. They were like a mustard seed when you compare them to what was happening in their day.

How do you explain the kingdom of heaven to twelve followers and get them excited about it? Remember, the kingdom is not about what the disciples thought. Just like today the kingdom of God is not about what we as believers think it is, or what we think it can accomplish, or what we think it can do. The kingdom of God is initiated by God Himself. When God initiates something it is very powerful. He may initiate it with you as an individual, or He may initiate something in His kingdom with your Sunday school class, or your family, or a few of your friends. Pay attention, if God initiated it, He will see it through. And it will develop into something much larger than you can imagine.

In order for a mustard seed to develop into something larger there has to be proper nurture. You cannot develop the kingdom of God with twelve disciples who do not believe. There had to be something of deep substance within those twelve if this message was ever going to spread and develop. Today there are literally millions of people across this earth who gather on Sunday mornings to worship the One true God.

Can you imagine all of these people at church to worship someone they never met physically?

In this passage Jesus was physically teaching those twelve misfits how to operate in the kingdom. Can you imagine getting such an assignment? Suppose Jesus said to you, "I will give you thirty days and here is your message. I want you to change your whole state in thirty days."

We would probably first ask, "How much money do I have to spend?"

Just look at society today and you will see millions being spent by people just to try and get others to believe their message. Money will not convince people. Building the kingdom of God requires kingdom resources.

God chooses to build His kingdom using us. Jesus did a great job with the twelve. What else could explain that two thousand years later our lives have been changed by Him and we gather to worship Him? How do you put together that kind of kingdom? There has to be proper nourishment. God was about to help these disciples focus on His vision of the kingdom instead of their vision of what they thought they could do. We cannot initiate or accomplish this task, but God chooses to do it through us. He was beginning to help His disciples see that they have to do something more than just be with Him physically. They must have a connection with Him.

This is the message that God shared with the false prophets in Jeremiah 23:16: "They speak a vision of their own heart, not from the mouth of the Lord."

The words and ways of man will never nourish and grow the kingdom of God. Too many want to be Christians without spending time in a close connection with Christ. They want to appear to have a close connection, but they do not want to pay the price for developing a close connection with Christ.

Jesus gives greater meaning to life and His kingdom to those who spend time with Him in private. Understand, public worship will not substitute for private devotion. You cannot go to church on Sunday and think you are going to give God all your worship when your private life does not match up. The way in which you participate in the kingdom of God is directly related to how much time you spend in private devotion behind the scenes with the Lord Jesus. What do you know about Jesus this week that you did not know last week? What did you learn in your private time with Him?

There is a mindset in our day that believes success in the kingdom means that there must be large crowds of people in a church hearing the message. Many say that in order to be successful as a follower of Christ, you must share the message with the masses. This is not what Christ taught His disciples. Christ shared ALL things when the disciples were alone with Him. He started with twelve. Our success in the kingdom of God is directly related to the connection we share with Jesus Christ. This connection is established through private one-on-one time with Him.

In the book of Jeremiah there are many instances where God brought a Word to Jeremiah in private so that he might share with His people in public. God told Jeremiah that he would share the message but no one would listen. With the mindset of our current world we would have to say that Jeremiah was unsuccessful in the kingdom of God. However, the kingdom of God does not hinge on man's mindset of success. In order to have any understanding of God's kingdom a believer must spend time alone with God to seek His Heart and His Mind. Until our hearts and minds are lined up with Christ, we simply are not connected. This connection develops deeper as we continue to spend time alone with Christ in the Word of God.

Peter believed in Jesus and was close to Him. What Peter did not believe was that he was capable of denying Christ. Jesus knew that he would deny Him because He knew Peter's heart. Even though Peter messed up, Peter believed in Jesus. Jesus was not looking at what Peter was at the time, He was looking at what He would shape Him to be. This shaping happens in our time alone with Jesus. When God saved Alison from those house fires, He knew that one day He would save her so that she would know Him. As He drew her, He began to shape her. Through this shaping He continues to draw her closer and deepen the connection. He did this for me, Elaine, and Alison's mom, and He will do this to all who receive Him.

Shaping like this takes place in private times with Jesus. People are afraid to be close to God because they are afraid of what it will reveal about themselves. It was not until Peter saw for himself what his heart was capable of that he was deeply sorry. For Christians, it is not until we see our sin through God's eyes that we are deeply sorry. In Peter's private time with Jesus, He revealed to Peter that He would deny Him. When Peter denied Him, the Word spoken by Jesus in private came back to his memory immediately.

There will always be a denial. Self is a strong and powerful source that desires to fulfill the flesh and be righteous apart from Christ. It is human nature to protect self. When the pressure was on, Peter chose to protect himself. When self is exalted, Christ is denied. When Christ is exalted, self is denied. The only way to exalt Christ over self is to spend private time with Him. Exalting self will never profit the kingdom of God. Choosing to deny self is the only way one will ever experience what it means to walk in the Spirit. This kind of living is what Jesus meant when He said, "I have come that they may have life, and that they may have it more abundantly" (John 10:10).

Making a connection with Christ means to pursue His Mind, His Heart, His Way, and His Desire. The mind of Christ is not attained by simply spending two days of sitting with Him in private. It requires developing a consistent time with Him to get to know His Mind. Jesus taught all twelve of His disciples apart from the crowds. But Scripture reveals that there were three disciples who spent more time with Him than the others: the three were Peter, James, and John. In the previous chapter Peter's relationship with Christ was discussed in great detail. Let's take a look at the relationship between James and Jesus.

Jesus Calls James

> *Going on from there, He saw two other brothers, James the son of Zebedee, and John his brother, in the boat with Zebedee their father, mending their nets. He called them, and immediately they left the boat and their father, and followed Him.*
>
> **Matthew 4:21-22**

From that time on, James is mentioned on a few occasions as being one of the three that Jesus took on special assignments apart from the twelve. One of those times was when Jesus was transfigured on the mount.

Now after six days Jesus took Peter, James, and John his brother, led them up on a high mountain by themselves; and He was transfigured before them. His face shone like the sun, and His clothes became as white as the light. And behold, Moses and Elijah appeared to them, talking with Him...While he was still speaking, behold, a bright cloud overshadowed them; and suddenly a voice came out of the cloud, saying, "This is My beloved Son, in whom I am well pleased. Hear Him!"

Matthew 17:1-3, 5

There are many things about Jesus that even these three men did not understand. What stands out though, is that when called by Jesus, James immediately left the boat and his father and followed Him. It is important to take a look at what Jesus was teaching His disciples just before He took Peter, James, and John on the mountain by themselves.

Then Jesus said to His disciples, "If anyone desires to come after Me, let him deny himself, and take up his cross, and follow Me. For whoever desires to save his life will lose it, but whoever loses his life for My sake will find it.

Matthew 16:24-25

What a message to share right before He took Peter, James, and John on the mountain to experience Him in a much deeper way! After the disciples fell on their faces afraid for what they had witnessed,

...Jesus came and touched them and said, "Arise, and do not be afraid." When they had lifted up their eyes, they saw no one but Jesus only.

Now as they came down from the mountain, Jesus commanded them, saying, "Tell the vision to no one until the Son of Man is risen from the dead."

Matthew 17:7-9

Jesus had already shared with His disciples that,

...He must go to Jerusalem, and suffer many things from the elders and chief priests and scribes, and be killed, and be raised the third day.

Matthew 16:21

Jesus taught His disciples all they needed to know for the moment. Yet, it is clear that there were still things that they did not understand. They were learning the ways of God. While there were some difficult truths to understand, James was included as one of the disciples who Jesus took behind the scene for a private time of instruction. One thing that is clear about James, is that when Jesus called, he immediately followed. He dropped his way of life and followed after Jesus.

Why would Jesus teach about self-denial just before He took the three on the mountain? Because God cannot trust the truths of the kingdom to those who desire to live for self and not for God. God's desire for His children is for the best, and His best lies in kingdom living. God is not requesting you leave your best life to follow a life of drudgery, He is requesting that you leave the mediocrity in this world for the riches of Christ in the kingdom. His goal is abundant living in Him. In order to accomplish a deeper connection with Him there must be a desire to live for Him and not for self.

The desires of self do not line up with the truth of the kingdom. It is clear that on several occasions the disciples were relying on their own understanding rather than on Christ's wisdom. Without a connection with Christ there will be no connection to the Voice of God. A truth from God's Word could be happening right before your eyes, and you could miss it if there is no daily connection.

Remember when Jesus was coming into Jerusalem on a donkey and the people were waving branches and shouting Hosanna? They were lifting Him up, rejoicing, and having a wonderful time. You know what Jesus was doing? He was weeping over Jerusalem. They were close to Jesus but had no real connection to know what was going on in the kingdom. Most of those people that were waving branches singing hosanna were not at the cross! They had a public connection but not a close one. It was not real. It was not intimate.

One day Jesus was walking down the street and there was a multitude of people around Him. They were pressing in on Him. People wanted to touch Him and wanted to be next to Him. They wanted it to be known that they had a public connection with Jesus. They were not at the cross though. Jesus was walking along with all those people around Him. He looked over and saw a man in a tree, and do you know what Jesus did? He took all His focus from that public group and went over to that one man and told him He wanted to go home with him. Why? When Jesus was walking through His public ministry, He knew how many around Him would never make a real connection. He knew that in the kingdom it would start small with a few who really cared. The kingdom would blossom from there. He could have stayed in the limelight with all of those people but no, He turned to one man. Jesus saw the Father at work in that man and knew there was something real and personal that this man wanted. Zacchaeus wanted to be involved with this man named Jesus. Jesus spent the day with him and changed his life. How about you?

Burning Thought #7

Focus on Christ

On December 21, 2016 I began my devotional time going through the book of Jeremiah. It is amazing how God speaks to us in the private times we spend with Him. Look at my journal entry!

March 10, 2017: Jeremiah 33:3

Today Elaine and I fly to Atlanta to look for a new house! Excited and challenged. Amazing that God saved this verse for me for today, seeing I started through this incredible book in December 2016.

> *Call to Me, and I will answer you, and show you great and mighty things, which you do not know.*
> ### Jeremiah 33:3

Elaine and I were praying about finding a house in Georgia for the purpose of moving and establishing *Think LifeChange Institute of Biblical Counseling*. We lived in The Woodlands, Texas. We needed to reduce our cost of living. In order to do this, we needed to downsize our home and move to a less expensive place to live. We knew that we would have to live off the equity of a home we would sell. After searching the internet for homes, we traveled to Georgia to begin the house search. God had provided an amazing godly realtor to help us in the process.

We looked at a great number of homes but nothing in our price range fit what we needed. We were tired and almost hopeless. Then the realtor said, "I have one other home I would like you to see. It is not on the market. Friends of mine have just made a decision to sell and no one else knows about this home. Is it okay to go there?"

Immediately, this passage came to mind, *"Call to Me, and I will answer you, and show you great and mighty things, **which you do not know**.* Amazing! God not only saved this verse for me in my quiet time but showed us a house that we did not know about! It was not even on the market yet! We placed a contract on it on March 11, 2017! It has been a perfect place for us!

Focus on Self

Can you imagine the disaster that would come if a person was unwilling to allow this verse to penetrate the heart?

Call to Me, and I will answer you, and show you great and mighty things, which you do not know.

Jeremiah 33:3

If you do not call on God daily, He will not answer you, and you will not see great and mighty things which you are already blind to. If self were the focus, instead of calling on God, Elaine and I may have found a home and missed out on the perfect one we needed for following God. Please do not ever assume that your way will be better than what God has planned for you. But, you will never know His Way if you do not spend time with Him in private.

Chapter Eight

God's Voice: Seen or Behind the Scene

Then the word of the LORD came to me, saying...Therefore prepare yourself and arise, and speak to them all that I command you.

Jeremiah 1:4, 17

It is no secret that people desire to be seen, to be noticed, and to be heard. While not all people have a desire to be in the spotlight, it is evident that all people desire to be noticed in some way.

Over the course of several years, we have heard many people say that they do not feel heard, appreciated, or noticed. Some say, "Well, nobody knows me. I'm a behind-the-scenes person." But do you have a desire to be known as the best at something in your circle of friends or in your family? Maybe you want to be known as the best dad, mom, grandma, teacher, friend, or mentor.

While traveling to conferences, Kerry witnessed many firsthand experiences of people's desire to be seen. Many times, he would meet and counsel with people that were down and out or depressed. An hour later, he might see those same people in the presence of the keynote speaker with smiles on their faces desiring the speaker to sign a book. It was amazing to see the change of countenance on their faces from the counseling room to the presence of a poplar person–it seemed as though they were transformed.

Selfish Ambition

Everyone struggles with selfish ambition. By very nature of being human, we want attention. People want to make a name for themselves in some area of life. People want to be seen, they want to be heard, and they want things their own way all the time. Have you noticed that? Selfish ambition drives us to seek attention for ourselves. We feel we must be the center of attention. People with selfish ambition do not listen well, they simply want to be heard. They are really not interested in what others are saying. And it was no different in Jesus' day.

This was the case for the Pharisees. The Pharisees had made a name for themselves in the religious world. They were the ones who the people turned to for knowledge in regard to God's law. They were looked up to and respected. The sad thing is that when God (Jesus) was standing right in front of them, they did not recognize Him. Why? They had no connection with God. They had a bigger interest in being seen rather than in spending time with God behind the scene. They were in the religious scene but completely missed the activity of God. Jesus spoke to them saying, "But you do not have His word abiding in you, because whom He sent, Him you do not believe" (John 5:38). We established in earlier chapters that Jesus was the "word that became flesh" (John 1:14). Yet, they did not know Him, and eventually sent Him to the cross to be crucified. Jesus threatened their desire to make a name for themselves.

Jesus said to them,

> *I do not receive honor from men. But I know you, that you do not have the love of God in you. I have come in My Father's name, and you do not receive Me; if another comes in his own name, him you will receive. How can you believe, who receive honor from one another, and do not seek the honor that comes from the only God?*
> **John 5:41-44**

To live a life making a name for Christ is to live a life where you are behind the scene. You may not receive any praise from men. In fact, you may be despised by men just like Jesus was despised. The goal is to honor the Lord and not men. As a Christian, we are to put Christ on display, not self. This means being content in your heart to receive approval only from God and not looking to receive praise from people. Christ is the Savior! We are to share Him with those needing salvation and freedom from sin. We are to exalt Him and place self behind the scene. This is only accomplished by spending meaningful time making a connection with Jesus in an intimate love relationship. Allowing people to see Christ in you will never happen when you love self more than God. When stepping onto the scene as a representative of Christ, people must see Him and not you. There is no room for selfish ambition while representing Christ.

The intent of the people in Jesus' day was to make a name for themselves, not a name for God. That can happen in our lives as a group of people or it can happen in your life as an individual. It can also happen in families. A family may want to make a name for themselves so everybody will know about their great family. It can happen as a schoolteacher. A teacher may want to be known as the best teacher. Of course you should take pride in your work. You should give the best that you have as though you are doing the work for the Lord. But you can also develop selfish ambition in that area of your life.

God dealt with Kerry about selfish ambition in a very intense way years ago. Below is what God taught him.

Kerry

When Elaine and I left First Baptist Church of West Palm Beach to move to Atlanta, Georgia, on a new assignment from God, I was absolutely amazed. First of all, I was not looking for a new position. I was absolutely shocked when I received a call from Dr. Henry Blackaby. He said, "Kerry, God has given me a new assignment with Southern Baptists in the area of revival and spiritual awakening. I'm going to be representing three of our national agencies and I'm wondering if you would come and serve with me. We'll be responsible for the U.S. and Canada."

I was not looking for that position, and at the same time, God had given me an assignment when I was in West Palm to begin writing with Dr. Henry Brandt. I never wanted to write a book in my life. I thought I did enough writing in college and seminary for a lifetime. But God uniquely gave me a new assignment.

After moving to Atlanta, we were trying to get the book called *The Heart of the Problem* published. Publishing is a difficult industry to get into and I tried everything I knew, but it seemed like the publisher just was not interested. I thought, "Why are they not interested? This is a message that God gave us. Why wouldn't they be interested in what God gave us?"

On a visit to Nashville, Tennessee, in January 1995, I was in a prayer meeting with some very godly people. They didn't know what was going on in my heart. That morning in my quiet time I read the passage in Genesis 11 about the tower of Babel.

> Now the whole earth had one language and one speech. And it came to pass, as they journeyed from the east, that they found a plain in the land of Shinar, and they dwelt there. Then they said to one another, "Come, let us make bricks and bake them thoroughly. They had brick for stone, and they had asphalt for mortar. And they said, "Come, let us build ourselves a city, and a tower whose top is in the heavens; let us make a name for ourselves....
>
> **Genesis 11:1-4**

Then God said, "Kerry, your problem is selfish ambition." The moment God began to show me myself, I begin to tell Him why I was really not that bad after all. While kneeling there in that prayer meeting I said, "Well, God, you know I've always been a guy behind the scenes. I've always been the one helping someone else. My wife even knows that I don't have to be the center of attention. I don't have to be under the lights. I don't have to be on the platform. God, I don't need to have that kind of attention. God, I don't see myself as having all this selfish ambition that You seem to be bringing to my mind right now."

I began to reason about how I could measure selfish ambition in my life. All these thoughts went through my head quickly: a lot happened in just a few minutes. I was imagining a scale from 0 to 10. If 0 meant you had no selfish ambition in your life and 10 meant you had as much as anybody ought to have, where would you put yourself on the scale?

That is what I pictured as I said to God, "God, I don't have as much selfish ambition as other people." Have you ever said something like that? If you find somebody else worse than you, you'll feel better about yourself. I said, "On a scale of 0–10, I can't be more than a 2!"

I'll never forget what God impressed on my mind when I said that. He said, "Kerry, I've called you to be My servant. You're here to bring honor to My Name–not yours. If 2 is all you have, then 2 is too much if you want to be My servant."

I didn't like that answer at all! While on my knees in that room I prayed and asked God to forgive me. I said, "Oh, God, I know that I'll probably have a struggle with this again, but Lord, You are right. I really wanted that first book published because it would have been nice to have my name on a book. God, I want to ask You to forgive me. That was so wrong of me and Lord, if You will forgive me and cleanse me, I'll devote the rest of my life to try and make a name for You."

It is so amazing that when you get right with God, He then accomplishes His work in you. Not only did that book get published, but He also showed me what He could do when I would get out of the way. Two months earlier, I had sent a fresh manuscript to that same publisher on a different subject. I sent it right after Thanksgiving. They were closed two weeks at the end of December. They could not have had our manuscript more than two weeks. The first book took three years to be published.

But after I repented, I got up from that prayer meeting, walked across the street in downtown Nashville, and went in to see the editors. They said, "Kerry, we didn't know you were in town. We just had a meeting about you and Dr. Brandt's book that you sent to us a couple of months ago and made a decision this morning. We're ready to sign a contract with you right now."

You know what God said to me? "Kerry, when you get out of the way, it doesn't take Me long to accomplish things."

It is amazing how selfish ambition can seep into any area of life. It is easy to move to a position of wanting to make a name for yourself instead of for God.

What about you? Is there any area in your life where God needs to deal with selfish ambition? Selfish ambition is a very serious sin against God. He is Holy. He is God. He has purchased us as His children—with His own blood. We are bought with a price. Our whole existence is to glorify Him in our body, our mind, and our soul.

Some will say, "Well, you need selfish ambition to get ahead in this world."

As a child of God, the goal of life is not to get ahead according to the world's standard; it is to continuously grow in the love we have for Jesus and then share all that God gives us to others. The purpose of writing the books that Dr. Brandt and I wrote was to teach and help others learn how to live this kind of life–a life free from the bondage of sin. If my desire moves to wanting to make a name for myself then I just robbed God of all that He has taught me to teach others. God provided the insight and direction for these books. For me to desire to make a name for myself using what God revealed to us behind the scenes is stealing from God. Even the world recognizes that as plagiarism. The danger lies in the fact that when we fall into the temptation of selfish ambition we fall into confusion and the wisdom from above cannot be seen any longer.

Later that week, I was reading in the Scripture during another quiet time in James chapter 3.

> *But if you have bitter envy and self-seeking in your hearts, do not boast and lie against the truth. This wisdom does not descend from above, but is earthly, sensual, demonic. For where envy and self-seeking exist, confusion and every evil thing are there.*
> **James 3:14-16**

All things that come to us are from God and for His glory. God is not the author of confusion. God does not author confusion but He will bring confusion to us based on our disobedience. He will allow us to be confused. He's not the author of it–our sin is the author of the confusion.

But God desires a relationship with you and He makes you dependent on Him. We should not want others to know who we are–we should want them to know who God is. When God gets all of the attention, others will take notice. The world is tired of seeing what we can do as an individual, family, or church because they can duplicate most of our events. Many of the events we do as a church, the world can do a little bit better. But when they hear of something happening that only God can do, it gets their attention.

This is what the Lord was revealing about the false prophets in Jeremiah 23.

> *Thus says the LORD of hosts: "Do not listen to the words of the prophets who prophesy to you. They make you worthless; they speak a vision of their own heart, not from the mouth of the LORD. They continually say to those who despise Me, "The*

LORD has said, 'You shall have peace'"; and to everyone who walks according to the dictates of his own heart, they say, "No evil shall come upon you.'"

Jeremiah 23:16-17

They were speaking their own words and saying that God said it. If we are promoting anything in the church that is not what the Lord has directed the entire church is in danger of being in total confusion. Man cannot produce the wisdom of God. The wisdom of God comes from above to those who walk in a connection to Jesus.

To be part of a wonderful church that is seeing wonderful success can bring you to the most dangerous avenue of life. It is not when you are in the valley that you fall down and are hurt severely–it is when you are on the mountain top.

When you are walking with God, you may be on the mountaintop, but if you turn to selfish ambition, He will bring confusion and you will begin to fall. When you fall off the mountaintop, it's a long way down and when you hit–it hurts.

As gently and as kindly as we know how to share–selfish ambition is from hell. It is not from God. God wants to cleanse us so that from this day forward we can say, "Oh, God, please do not let us make a name for ourselves. Use us in such a way, that what is seen will bring honor and glory to Your Name."

What about your individual life, your family life, your corporate life, or your school life? Do you want God to reign so strongly that selfish ambition would be removed from your life? If so, then people around you will notice there is something distinctly different in your life, and it does not have to do with self.

This is true for the woman in Mark 5:24-31.

> *So Jesus went with him, and a great multitude followed Him and thronged Him. Now a certain woman had a flow of blood for twelve years, and had suffered many things from many physicians. She had spent all that she had and was no better, but rather grew worse. When she heard about Jesus, she came behind Him in the crowd and touched His garment. For she said, "If only I may touch His clothes, I shall be made well."*

Immediately the fountain of her blood was dried up, and she felt in her body that she was healed of the affliction. And Jesus, immediately knowing in Himself that power had gone out of Him, turned around in the crowd and said, "Who touched My clothes?"

But His disciples said to Him, "You see the multitude thronging You, and You say, 'Who touched Me?'"

Who touched Me? The disciples must have thought that was a crazy question. Jesus was surrounded by a great crowd and asked, "Who touched Me?" After the woman came forward and told Him the whole truth He said to her,

"Daughter, your faith has made you well. Go in peace, and be healed of your affliction."
Mark 5:34

Jesus highlighted the woman's faith. The woman had a sincere heart to believe that touching Jesus' garment would heal her. Jesus can tell the difference between someone who is sincere and wants a relationship and someone who just wants to be seen in the crowd next to Him. The disciples were right next to Jesus but missed the activity of God. What could cause us to miss the activity of Him? To want to be seen and known instead of making Him known. He must increase and we must decrease.

Behind the scene with God, have you ever heard Him say to you, "Is it enough for you to have a relationship with Me if no one ever saw anything you ever did?" Maybe no one ever recognized you or complemented you. Is it enough that you have a personal and real connection with Jesus regardless of what is going on around you? Are you interested in being seen with Jesus, or being behind the scene with Jesus in a personal relationship with Him?

If you step onto the scene without first being with Jesus behind the scene, then you place yourself in danger. Your time in the counsel of the Lord is your protection in the kingdom of God. This was true for Jeremiah. God told Jeremiah that He would give him a message but no one would listen to him. God had to be enough for Jeremiah. God spoke to him that he had to be completely dependent on the Word of the Lord. He had to take the time behind the scene to spend with God.

Do you want to be great in the kingdom? Do you know what you are asking? Your protection when you step into an assignment for the kingdom of God is Jesus. If you do not spend time with Jesus behind the scene in a love relationship, you will step on the scene and fall into all the traps that are set before you. Does not God's Word burn like a fire in our hearts? When we are in close connection to God, our hearts are tender to the Word. Our hearts are purified by its cleansing power. Take advantage of the time you have to spend behind the scene with God. Being seen will not provide the life-changing power that sitting in the presence of the Lord will provide. Do you want to be seen as someone who knows Jesus, or do you want to have a deep personal connection with Him? It is your choice.

Burning Thought #8

*Then the word of the LORD came to me, saying...Therefore pre-
pare yourself and arise, and speak to them all that I command
you.*

Jeremiah 1:4, 17

Focus on Christ

Has God ever revealed something in His Word that you didn't want
to do? When He does, then preparation for the task ahead is the next
step. You must saturate your mind in the Word of God to gain a proper
perspective. When God's Word is absolutely clear to you, it is time to
respond obediently. Waiting is no longer an option, action is the answer.

If you chose not to obey the Word, it is likely because you fear how
people will respond if you follow God's direction. You think you will
look like an outsider if you do something others are not willing to do.
Guess what? You will! You will look like Jesus who always stood out
in a crowd. When the Voice of God speaks through His Word, carry out
what He says without doubting or fear. I find that when the Word is in
your heart, it burns like a fire and will not let you go! You must speak!
Resistance at this point takes more energy than simply obeying.

You should fear God if you are unwilling to carry out what He says.
Do not waste time trying to decide what to do when you know the truth.
The great antidote for a fear of people is a healthy fear of God. Jeremiah thought he could not speak for the Lord because he was so young
and inexperienced. He was afraid people would not respect him. Age
doesn't matter when God is the one giving the assignment. God wanted
him to have confidence in Him, not his personal abilities. Where is your
confidence? In Christ, or in your skills?

Focus on Self

Self is the greatest roadblock to speaking on God's behalf. As long as
you are worried about self, you will not exalt Christ.

If you want to experience what any other person on earth experiences,
you probably will. But wouldn't you rather experience something that
is not of this world? Something that contains the unsearchable riches of
Christ? You can, but it is only available through a deep walk with God!

Chapter Nine

God's Voice: Inner or Outer Circle

Then the LORD said to me, "You have seen well, for I am ready to perform My word.

Jeremiah 1:12

There are all kinds of influential circles today. In our lives we may have a small group of people who would be considered our inner circle. We can also have an even smaller inner circle from that group consisting of one or two people. We all have an inner circle and an outer circle in our relationships. There are some groups where we share the intents of our heart and other groups we do not. These different levels of relationships are determined by which people fit in the ones that we choose. We choose who will be in our inner circle. Jesus chose twelve men to be in His inner circle. But He also chose three whom He would pull aside and share even deeper truths.

Most of us tend to have an intimate relationship with only a few. Is Jesus a part of one of your few intimate relationships? Do you share the details and intents of your heart with Him? Few in Jesus' day had a close spiritual connection with Him. Many simply wanted to appear they were close and so they sought opportunities to be physically close to Him in public. You can worship God publicly in a group but worship can go to a deeper level in the private experience with Jesus. He is looking for people who will make the effort to get alone with Him in private. Those are the people who He develops into His inner circle of disciples. There are negative sides to inner circles and there are positive sides.

Kerry

God has given me opportunity to counsel some pastors in our country who are well known to many. In fact if I wrote their names, you would probably know them. These pastors were having a difficult time in their lives and wanted help. Due to the fact that they were well known, there was no one in their community who they wanted to turn to because they desired to keep the difficulty private. Yet, they knew they needed some biblical counsel. In counseling some of these leaders I discovered that many do not desire to be better, they just desire to appear or feel better. Do you know that some people do not desire to have a better marriage, they just want to appear to have a better marriage? Some people do not desire to have a close connection with Jesus, they just want to appear to have a close connection with Him.

You may know people who do not want anything to do with anybody else outside of their small group. These groups of people would be considered cliques. This is considered the negative side of an inner circle. People who exclude others from their inner circle of friends and are unwilling to develop any other relationships are not healthy. This is not the desire God has for us in relationships.

The positive side of an inner circle is that there are some deep spiritual things that happen in this group that does not tend to happen in the general public. To keep it positive, you must not exclude other people from all activities in your life. If you did, you would go against the very thing that Jesus commanded, "A new commandment I give to you, that you love one another..." (John 13:34). A proper inner circle will develop into relationships with people who will help you in desperate times of need. People outside this inner circle cannot give you the same kind of help as those in your close connection of spiritual friends.

In chapter 8, we discussed a scene in the book of Mark where Jesus was in a crowd and a woman touched His garment because she desired healing. She touched just the hem of His garment and Jesus said, "who touched Me?" Jesus knew who touched Him but desired to make a close connection with her.

While He was still speaking, some came from the ruler of the synagogue's house who said, "Your daughter is dead. Why trouble the Teacher any further?"

As soon as Jesus heard the word that was spoken, He said to the ruler of the synagogue, "Do not be afraid; only believe." And He permitted no one to follow Him except Peter, James, and John the brother of James.

Mark 5:35-37

Jesus also had an inner circle of twelve disciples. Most of Jesus' time was spent with those twelve key people. He taught them apart from the large crowds. He shared truths with the twelve that He did not share with the crowds. He spent most of His time with those twelve performing ministry needs to the hurting and needy.

One of those twelve was Judas, the one who would betray Jesus. How would you like to have Judas in your inner circle? When we are selecting our inner circle do we say, "O Lord, help me to find a Judas?" No! Yet Jesus knew exactly who He was selecting for His inner circle.

I know whom I have chosen; but that the Scripture may be fulfilled...

John 13:18

It was key that Jesus knew intimately who was in His inner circle. He knew Judas was there and He knew what Judas was going to do. He did not try to remove him from His group. He just continued to do what the Heavenly Father had called Him to do.

In Mark 5:35-37 we see that Jesus is presented with a desperate need. that called Him to a secluded place. He permitted no one to follow Him except Peter, James, and John. This is yet another account of Jesus pulling aside the same three men. We have revealed in the previous chapters some other instances where Jesus pulled these men apart from the twelve. As we read these instances it is important to ask ourselves this question, "Am I in the inner circle with Jesus?"

You might say you are in the group like the five thousand on the hillside where Jesus taught. Some of you might think that you have developed and grown in your life to be in a circle of twelve. Or, would you put yourself close to Jesus but not sure you would be one of the three?

When a desperate need came, Jesus took three with Him. Can you imagine Jesus physically walking into the back of your church on Sunday morning? Imagine for a moment Him physically walking in your church and crying out to the congregation saying, "There is a desperate need and I need three of you to go with Me for this need." Would He call your name? You might say yes, it would be me. If you think that is so, you are probably not in the right position yet. Jesus looks at the heart of people. He does not look at success, finances, how many people you know, how large your business has grown in the past twenty years, or how many Sunday school lessons you have taught. He looks at you and He sees what is in your heart. He knew the hearts of Peter, James, and John. He took His inner circle with Him. Would you be on that inner circle if Jesus came today?

Jesus sees things in us that others do not. Jesus knew what would take place in the lives of Peter, James, and John. He knew whether they would glorify God or not. We have learned about the relationship that Jesus had with Peter and James. Now we will examine Jesus' relationship with John.

John: The Disciple Whom Jesus Loved

Jesus called John to follow Him at the same time that He called James. John and James were brothers:

> Going on from there, He saw two other brothers, James the son of Zebedee, and John his brother, in the boat with Zebedee their father, mending their nets. He called them, and immediately they left the boat and their father, and followed Him.
> **Matthew 4:21-22**

John was one of the three disciples Jesus called on for special assignments. He was also referenced as the one Jesus loved:

> Now there was leaning on Jesus' bosom one of His disciples, whom Jesus loved.
> **John 13:23**

And again on a later account after Mary Magdalene found Jesus' tomb empty,

Then she ran and came to Simon Peter, and to the other disciple, whom Jesus loved, and said to them, "They have taken away the Lord out of the tomb, and we do not know where they have laid Him."

John 20:2

And again, Jesus revealed Himself the third time after He was raised from the dead.

Then Peter, turning around, saw the disciple whom Jesus loved following...

John 21:20

While we know that Jesus loves all, we recognize that He had a special connection with John. He was in the inner circle with Jesus and Jesus shared things with him separate from the twelve. It is also evident that John showed a special affection toward Jesus. The Scripture reveals how John leaned on His breast at the supper when Jesus was sharing how one of the twelve would betray Him.

Now there was leaning on Jesus' bosom one of His disciples, whom Jesus loved. Simon Peter therefore motioned to him to ask who it was of whom He spoke...Then, leaning back on Jesus' breast, he said to Him, "Lord, who is it?"

John 13:23-25

One of the greatest recognitions in regard to John's love for Christ is that he was the only disciple who was at the cross with Jesus:

Now there stood by the cross of Jesus His mother, and His mother's sister, Mary the wife of Clopas, and Mary Magdalene. When Jesus therefore saw His mother, and the disciple whom He loved standing by, He said to His mother, "Woman, behold your son!" Then He said to the disciple, "Behold your mother!" And from that hour that disciple took her to his own home.

John 19:25-27

As we look at the relationship John had with Jesus, and the fact that he was the only disciple at the cross, a challenging question is posed to disciples today. A question that none could answer with complete confidence, yet, one that will challenge the love that we possess for our Lord and Savior Jesus Christ.

Would you go to the cross with the One you love?

This is a question that is impossible to answer until you are in that situation. Alison ran through fire for her mom. But would she go to the cross with Jesus? That question may never be answered but the love that we have for our Savior needs to be discussed. It is clear that Jesus loves the whole world. He laid down His life for all. Many question God's love but God's love is not in question. He answered that when He gave His only Son for all who will repent and turn to Him. While we may never know if we would go to the cross with Jesus, we can answer whether or not we are willing to surrender our entire life for the love of Jesus Christ. God knows our hearts. He is not looking for perfect people. He is interested in those with a willing heart who will follow Him.

Willing Hearts

As we learn a little more about Peter, James, and John, we see that we are not discussing people who had no faults. Would you have chosen Simon Peter to preach the first sermon in the New Testament? The one who denied Christ? Christ knew Simon Peter was going to deny Him, but He chose Him to be on the inner circle. Why? Because when Peter came to the realization of the wrongness he had done against His Lord, he turned immediately from his sin. He repented with great godly sorrow and was restored to a deeper relationship with Jesus. This is one of the keys to being on the inner circle with Christ. It is not about being perfect, but rather how quickly you respond to Him when He calls your name.

In learning more about these three men we realize that they were those kind of men. Men who were quick to turn to the Savior. Their desire was a close connection with Jesus. These three men wanted more than just to witness the activity of Jesus, they wanted a daily walk with Him. Their desire was to be His servants.

Yet with all of that being said, we see in Mark 14:50, "that they all forsook Him and fled." By the time Jesus reached the cross only one of these disciples was with Him. Being on the inner circle with Jesus does not mean you will never make a mistake. While you are to strive toward perfection you will sin while living on this earth. The key is not whether or not you sin, the key is how quickly you repent of your sin and get back into a right relationship with Christ. Remember, Peter denied Jesus. Does that mean that Jesus made a mistake in choosing Peter and putting him on His inner circle? Of course not. Did Peter make other mistakes? Absolutely. Jesus saw beyond what these men were and saw what they would become. Does Jesus do that with you? Are you glad that He does? Are you glad that He does not choose whether or not to have a relationship with you based on what you have accomplished? He looks into the heart. In these three men He saw what they would become not what they had done.

In the book of Jeremiah, God brings a Word to Jeremiah, not for him to keep it to himself, but for him to go and share the message with those whom God desired to hear it. God told Jeremiah that He was ready to perform His Word. The Holy Spirit does not share truths with us in our private time with Jesus in order for us to keep it in our inner circle.

Huddling in an inner circle to protect ourselves is not the goal. Jesus is crying out that He has come and put His Spirit within us. He came to teach us about love, joy, peace, gentleness, faithfulness, goodness, and self under the control of the Holy Spirit. This is not for our personal pleasure! Christ wants us strong to help strengthen others and take the message of Christ to others around us.

The Promise of the Holy Spirit

Jesus promised that when He left us He would provide a Helper.

> *"If you love Me, keep My commandments. And I will pray the Father, and He will give you another Helper, that He may abide with you forever—the Spirit of truth, whom the world cannot receive, because it neither sees Him nor knows Him; but you know Him, for He dwells with you and will be in you. I will not leave you orphans; I will come to you.*
>
> **John 14:15-18**

Jesus also said that He would provide the power of the Spirit to enable us to do what He assigned to us.

> *And being assembled together with them, He commanded them not to depart from Jerusalem, but to wait for the Promise of the Father, "which," He said, "you have heard from Me; for John truly baptized with water, but you shall be baptized with the Holy*

*Spirit not many days from now."...And they were all filled with
the Holy Spirit.*

Acts 1:4-5; 2:4

The gift that God provides to those who repent and believe is His
Spirit, the Holy Spirit. When a believer receives Jesus as their Lord and
Savior the Spirit of God takes up residence in that believer. Daily con-
sistent time with Jesus grows a believer and teaches them how to walk
in the Spirit of God and receive all the fruit of His Spirit in their lives.
God sent the Holy Spirit to the disciples after Jesus returned to heaven.
That same Spirit is available to every single Christian today. It was not
the disciples who had power. It was not that they were superhuman.
But the Spirit He placed within them was superhuman. The disciples
surrendered their lives to follow Jesus and spent one on one time with
Him. Why then do so many Christians live their lives defeated? Are
they spending one on one time with their Savior daily? God is ready to
perform His Word, but are His followers ready to receive it?

*These things I have spoken to you while being present with you.
But the Helper, the Holy Spirit, whom the Father will send in My
name, He will teach you all things, and bring to your remem-
brance all things that I said to you.*

John 14:25-26

The gift of the resurrection is the Spirit of God. God did not promise
an easy life but promised to send a treasure that He would place within
those who would receive it. This treasure provides all that is needed to
walk through whatever this life brings. The Spirit of God will place a
hunger in your heart for God's Word. The Father, the Son, and the Holy
Spirit do not operate outside of the Word of God. They are the Word of
God! To desire God is to desire His Word.

*[Abraham] He did not waver at the promise of God through un-
belief, but was strengthened in faith, giving glory to God, and
being fully convinced that what He had promised He was also
able to perform.*

Romans 4:20-21

Are Christians fully convinced that God is able to perform all that He
has promised? It seems for many that there is more unbelief in God's

ability than there is belief. It is dangerous as a Christian to live outside of the Word of God. It is past time that Christians stop living on the edge of faith and dive into the deep to be in Jesus' inner circle. Do you have any idea of the treasure that resides in a child of God?

Our Treasure

Kerry

I do not know about you, but there are many times in my life that I feel weak as a Christian. In fact, every time I stand up to speak to an audience, I feel weak. Every time I have the privilege of opening God's Word and talking to His precious people, I think, "Oh God, how can You use me?" I am a simple east Texas boy who grew up in a pastor's home. I grew up in small churches with 50 to 75 in attendance, and I never thought that I would ever be a member of a church, much less be on staff in a church that would have more than 100 in Sunday School. God has given me some awesome privileges since then to share His Word with His people. From my perspective, seeing who I am from the inside, I see the weakness of this vessel. Do any of you see a weakness in yourself as a vessel? We know Christ lives in us. Yet, though we know something about ourselves, our personality, the way in which we think, and the way we do things, we do not see ourselves necessarily as God sees us.

Years ago Elaine and I were in Fort Smith, Arkansas. I was leading a week long conference in a church. The pastor and his son came to greet us at our arrival in the airport. The son seemed to be in his thirties, had never been married, and was shy. He did not have the intellectual skills that many possess. Elaine and I were able to get to know him through the week as we were sharing at their church. He never really had much of a smile on his face, he never really stood out in a crowd, but he was always there to ask, "How can I help you?" When he would speak to me, I strained to hear him and tried to understand what he was saying. On Wednesday night of that week, Elaine and I went over to the pastor's daughter's home for a fellowship. The pastor, his wife, his daughter, and his son met us there. We had a good time together. At the end of our time together, the pastor said, "Kerry, we just want to take a moment and pray for one another, and we want to pray for you as you travel across the country and share this message God has given to you. We want to pray that God would use you in an awesome way."

There were several people that prayed that night, but there was only one person whose prayer I remember. It was the son's prayer. He began to pray, and as he did, he began to weep. He could barely get out his words. As he wept, Elaine and I began to weep. Then, the dad, mom, and sister were weeping. Here is what Phil prayed, "God, thank you for sending Kerry here this week, because he presented the truth in such a simple way that even I could understand it."

That broke my heart! God really does not care about what your skills are, He is concerned about how surrendered you are to Him. Shortly after we arrived home, I received an email from Phil. In fact, I received e-mails from him almost every week. Before Elaine and I left Arkansas I asked, "Phil, if God would lead you to, would you pray for me every week as I travel across the country and lead these conferences?"

Phil promised that he would. For years Phil wrote me e-mails and asked, "Where are you going to be this week, who are you going to be speaking to, I want to pray for you?"

Externally, Phil had a weak vessel, but he had the power of Christ living in him! Phil continues to be a prayer partner to this very day. I asked Phil if I could share this story and he happily agreed. God has used his story to inspire many others to depend on God for the ability to serve Him.

Jesus Christ is the Head of His Church. He is the King of your heart. He is the Savior of your salvation. He is the One who gives you hope and strength to go through whatever He allows in your life. He is more than capable of giving you the right direction for life. We are not without hope. The basis of our hope and the treasure of our heart is our Lord Jesus. But just how does Jesus work in and through us to be His ambassador to those around us?

Aroma of Christ

God makes you a distributor of the fragrance of His knowledge.

Now thanks be to God who always leads us in triumph in Christ, and through us diffuses the fragrance of His knowledge in every place.

2 Corinthians 2:14

It is God not us. That is a concept we must believe. He is the One, "who always leads us into triumph." As you read this, think back on your week. Maybe you went through some things that seemed as though there was no victory or triumph in it for you. I have had those kinds of minutes, days, and sometimes weeks, where I was not victorious. A weak vessel will never be spiritually victorious. I was trying to survive in my own strength and not in the strength of Christ. Paul goes on to say,

> *For we are to God the fragrance of Christ among those who are being saved and among those who are perishing. To the one we are the aroma of death leading to death, and to the other the aroma of life leading to life. And who is sufficient for these things?*
> **2 Corinthians 2:15-16**

In Paul's day when a general had conquered an area, there was always a triumphal march into the city. These triumphant marches were displays of the general's power. Coming into the city there would be two groups of captives marching in front of the general. There would be one group who had *voluntarily surrendered* to the general. These people gave up and said to the general, "We will be committed to you and will follow you now!"

There was another group marching in front of the general that came into this triumphal march. These were the ones who *held out* and were captured by force. They did not volunteer to surrender and continued to defy their situation by saying, "We will never follow this general!"

Right behind these captives, the general and his chariot, his horses, his strongest men, and his incense bearers marched. The incense bearers would burn massive amounts of incense throughout the parade. This strong aroma would dispense throughout the city, drifting up and down every street and alley. Wherever people walked, they would get a smell of the aroma. This smell was what reminded the people of the victory that the general achieved in battle.

As the general marched through the city, he displayed his trophies of war. To the ones who resisted the general and were captured, this aroma was the aroma of death. To those who had *voluntarily surrendered* in the battle, it was the aroma of victory. Tradition reveals that sometimes weeks later people would still get a hint of the aroma as they walked the streets. The incense was so strong that it had set in the minds of the people to remember the general who saved them, their victor! It is with this in mind that Paul said, "Thanks be to God who always leads us in triumph in Christ and through us defuses the fragrance of his knowledge in every place for we are to God the fragrance of Christ among those who are being saved."

The basis of our hope is not that we have in and of ourselves a fragrance that people want to smell. What Christ has done is put Himself in us so that when we live out our lives, others see Him working in us. The Scripture says we have this treasure, this hope, this foundation, this victory in Christ living within us as earthen vessels.

Earthen Vessels

In Chapter 4 we wrote about the potter and the clay from Jeremiah 18. We discussed how the potter takes clay and forms a vessel that He chooses based on His purposes for that vessel. In 2 Corinthians, the Apostle Paul shows that we are an earthen vessel, made of a material that is not of high value, but is very useful. Paul says we have this treasure within us as earthen vessels. You are God's special treasure, but He also puts a treasure within you.

> But we have this treasure in earthen vessels, that the excellence of the power may be of God and not of us. We are hard-pressed on every side, yet not crushed; we are perplexed, but not in despair; persecuted, but not forsaken; struck down, but not destroyed.

2 Corinthians 4:7-9

If you had a million dollars worth of jewelry, would you store it in a cardboard box and set it on the back porch? You would not do that at all. You would be afraid that someone would steal it. There may also be a concern of the elements, the weather, or maybe dirt or moisture causing some kind of film to form on the diamond or the gold, that would dull its brilliance. Rather, you would put a valuable treasure in a safe place where it would be protected.

It is absolutely amazing to me that God gave His only Son and said to us that He would put His Spirit in a simple earthen vessel like us! God places the treasure of His Son within all who say they will follow Him with all their heart, mind, and soul. Imagine God placing His presence and power in you so that whatever you face this week, the victory of Christ is always present. The fragrance of Christ is always within you to show Himself strong in your life. All the power of Christ is given to these old earthen vessels. For every person who is born again, God puts within him or her His Spirit. His Spirit is what brings power to life.

People go through all kinds of tragedies. God never said that you would never face difficulties. But as you face the difficulties, how will you respond? Are you easily crushed?

Have you ever broken a clay pot? It is very easy to do. I remember after Elaine and I moved to Florida, I took a big clay pot that had a little dirt and a small potted plant and moved it from an inside room to the patio. I thought it really looked nice. The next day the wind blew the plant over and the pot cracked. Earthen vessels are very susceptible to harm because they do not have much strength. It does not take a lot to destroy a clay pot. You can crush an empty clay pot with the power from your own hands. If you fill a clay pot with concrete, pressure will not crush the pot.

It is not because the outside of the clay vessel is so valuable and strong, it is what is on the inside that withstands the pressure. While we are earthen vessels, and in and of ourselves can be crushed, with Christ living in you there is power and strength. Christ is active and present in your life. The only reason you would not notice His presence or activity would be if you had a problem in your fellowship with Him. If you are in fellowship with Him, you will notice His activity in your life. You will understand how under the pressures of life–you will not be crushed. Paul does not say that you will not be pressed hard on. He does not say that you will not go through despairing times. He does not say that you will not have difficulty. What he says is that you have a treasure within you that will keep you from being destroyed.

A clay vessel is not of high value. Our bodies are not expensive but are extremely valuable to God's kingdom. God chose to work through us. God has a special treasure to store in us–His Son Jesus! To all who believe in Him and voluntarily surrender their life and chose to follow Him, He will place His treasure in you. That treasure provides power. If you depend on your own confidence, then you will fail in the Christian life. You cannot depend on the foundation of the future being bright based upon what you thought of the past. Our basis of hope has nothing to do with what happened in the past, it has everything to do with the power of God working in and through us today. We need to return to that kind of thinking.

Therefore we do not lose heart. Even though our outward man is perishing, yet the inward man is being renewed day by day. For our light affliction, which is but for a moment, is working for us a far more exceeding and eternal weight of glory, while we do not look at the things which are seen, but at the things which are not seen. For the things which are seen are temporary, but the things which are not seen are eternal.

2 Corinthians 4:16-18

You can be where you need to be with God. You can be renewed day by day with God if you choose to. Many of God's people have lost sight of eternal things. God did not create you for time; He created you for eternity. He placed within you His special treasure–the Lord Jesus–to accomplish eternal things while you are here on earth. In order to do this we must be simple earthen vessels that are usable for the Lord.

Before an earthen vessel can be used, it needs to be *clean*. You cannot be an earthen vessel with the treasure of Christ living in you and live an unholy life. Any area of disobedience in your life will keep you from being effective. God not only wants to work through you as an earthen vessel but He wants to work through a *clean* vessel. He also wants an *empty* vessel. We struggle all the time with self. But if you want to be used of God you need to be *empty* of self. Then you have to be *available* for service. God wants to use us in His kingdom work. We need to live in such a way that we have a confidence in the presence of God and not in our circumstances. Our confidence needs to be in the hidden treasure that is living within us. The power of Christ living within you. God uses clean, empty, available people!

Alison

My earthen vessel was burned by physical fire when I was 17 years old. Fire is an extremely powerful element that could have consumed and taken my earthen vessel off of this earth. At the time of the fires, I did not have the treasure of Christ living in me. God chose to save me from those fires and nine years later I received the gift of His hidden treasure, His Son living in me. God set a spiritual fire in my heart and has been fanning the flame over the past thirteen years. I have shared with you how the fire within has melted away the disobedience to God in my life.

Times of melting can be difficult. Today I thank my Lord and Savior that He loves me enough to burn away those temporary things that hold no eternal value. He now has cleansed me and emptied me to be a vessel that His power can work through. God's Word is the only fire that has the power to melt away the sinful things in our hearts that keep us from being in the inner circle with Jesus.

My spiritual growth over the past four years has been incredible. I owe it all to the Word of God living in me. For close to five years now I have not missed a day of a personal private time with my Savior. As the Lord has cleansed my heart more and more, I yearn for His Heart and His Righteousness. I crave His Word and cannot receive enough. I am here to share that this life is available to everyone who will yield to Him. Intimacy with Jesus is available to all who seek it. A hunger for His Word is available to all who ask for it and allow Him complete access to their heart. There has not been one area that God has cleansed in my life that I miss and want back. Not one temporary loss that has held a flame to the burning fire of the Spirit of God within. The love of Christ is of far more value than anything this world has to offer.

What Do You Seek?

What will you ask of Jesus today? Look at what the disciples did.

> *Again, the next day, John stood with two of his disciples. And looking at Jesus as He walked, he said, "Behold the Lamb of God!"*
>
> *The two disciples heard him speak, and they followed Jesus. Then Jesus turned, and seeing them following, said to them, "What do you seek?"*
>
> *They said to Him, "Rabbi" (which is to say, when translated, Teacher), "where are You staying?"*

He said to them, "Come and see." They came and saw where He was staying, and remained with Him that day (now it was about the tenth hour).

John 1:35-39

They desired to be with Him and see where He was staying. What do you seek from Jesus? To be seen in public with Him, to be on the scene with Him, or to be so close to Him in relationship and intimacy that you are in His inner circle spending private time with Him? The fire within my heart is present today because I desire to know my Savior as intimately as I possibly can. If I never do one more thing for the kingdom, it is enough for me to have the privilege to sit with the Son of God and commune with Him. There has been nothing more valuable than that in my life.

Kerry and I pray that God will use what He has taught us in private to ignite a spark in your heart that will yearn to read His Word and be with Him. We pray that you make the connection that the way to kingdom living is found in the Word of God.

God's Word is Like a Fire…

Burning Thought #9

Then the LORD said to me, "You have seen well, for I am ready to perform My word.

Jeremiah 1:12

Focus on Christ

What or who can you count on in your life? Sometimes people we thought we could count on simply do not follow through with what we were depending on them to do. Maybe our bank account did not fulfill our need. But you can always count on the promises of God. When God is ready to accomplish His Word, it cannot be slowed or restrained.

Jesus promised abundant living in John 10:10–*"I have come that they may have life, and that they may have it more abundantly."*

Jesus promised companionship in John 15:15–*"...but I have called you friends, for all things that I heard from My Father I have made known to you."*

God promised a renewal in Jeremiah 24:7–*"Then I will give them a heart to know Me, that I am the LORD; and they shall be My people, and I will be their God, for they shall return to Me with their whole heart."*

Jesus promised to fill our spiritual hunger in John 6:35–*"And Jesus said to them, "I am the bread of life. He who comes to Me shall never hunger, and he who believes in Me shall never thirst."*

God was watching to make sure His Word would come to pass. Whatever God begins, He finishes. In Philippians 1:6 the Scripture states, *"being confident of this very thing, that He who has begun a good work in you will complete it until the day of Jesus Christ."*

Focus on Self

In Jeremiah's day, God gave the people land and provisions, but they defiled the land by pursuing everything but God. How often does this happen to Christians? When God deals with us in a gracious manner, we are blessed, and when things are going well, we tend to defile what He has given us. To focus on self blinds us from the blessings of God. We need to praise God for His marvelous provisions, knowing that God has and will perform what He has said!